Barbiturates

DRUGS The Straight Facts

DRUGS
The Straight Facts

Barbiturates

Debra Henn
and Deborah DeEugenio

Consulting Editor
David J. Triggle

University Professor
School of Pharmacy and Pharmaceutical Sciences
State University of New York at Buffalo

CHELSEA HOUSE
PUBLISHERS
An imprint of Infobase Publishing

Barbiturates

Chelsea House
An imprint of Infobase Publishing
132 West 31st Street
New York NY 10001

Library of Congress Cataloging-in-Publication Data
Henn, Debra.
  Barbiturates / Debra Henn, Deborah de Eugenio ; David J. Triggle [series editor].
    p. cm. — (Drugs, the straight facts)
  Includes bibliographical references and index.
  ISBN 0-7910-8548-1 (hc : alk. paper)
  1. Barbiturates—Health aspects—Juvenile literature. 2. Drug abuse—Juvenile literature. I. DeEugenio, Deborah. II. Title.
RM325.H45 2007
615'.7821—dc22   2006027642

Chelsea House books are available at special discounts when purchased in bulk quantities for businesses, associations, institutions, or sales promotions. Please call our Special Sales Department in New York at (212) 967-8800 or (800) 322-8755.

You can find Chelsea House on the World Wide Web at http://www.chelseahouse.com

Text and cover design by Terry Mallon

Printed in the United States of America

Bang EJB 10 9 8 7 6 5 4 3 2 1

This book is printed on acid-free paper.

All links and Web addresses were checked and verified to be correct at the time of publication. Because of the dynamic nature of the Web, some addresses and links may have changed since publication and may no longer be valid.

Table of Contents

The Use and Abuse of Drugs

The issues associated with drug use and abuse in contemporary society are vexing subjects, fraught with political agendas and ideals that often obscure essential information that teens need to know to have intelligent discussions about how to best deal with the problems associated with drug use and abuse. *Drugs: The Straight Facts* aims to provide this essential information through straightforward explanations of how an individual drug or group of drugs works in both therapeutic and non-therapeutic conditions; with historical information about the use and abuse of specific drugs with discussion of drug policies in the United States; and with an ample list of further reading.

From the start, the series uses the word "drug" to describe psychoactive substances that are used for medicinal or non-medicinal purposes. Included in this broad category are substances that are legal or illegal. It is worth noting that humans have used many of these substances for hundreds, if not thousands of years. For example, traces of marijuana and cocaine have been found in Egyptian mummies; the use of peyote and Amanita fungi has long been a component of religious ceremonies worldwide; and alcohol production and consumption have been an integral part of many human cultures' social and religious ceremonies. One can speculate about why early human societies chose to use such drugs. Perhaps, anything that could provide relief from the harshness of life—anything that could make the poor conditions and fatigue associated with hard work easier to bear—was considered a welcome tonic. Life was likely to be, according to seventeenth century English philosopher Thomas Hobbes, "poor, nasty, brutish, and short." One can also speculate about modern human societies' continued use and abuse of drugs. Whatever the reasons, the consequences of sustained drug use are not insignificant—addiction, overdose, incarceration, and drug wars—and must be dealt with by an informed citizenry.

The problem that faces our society today is how to break the connection between our demand for drugs and the willingness of largely outside countries to supply this highly profitable trade. This is the same problem we have faced since narcotics and cocaine were outlawed by the Harrison Narcotic Act of 1914, and we have yet to defeat it despite current expenditures of approximately $20 billion per year on "the war on drugs." The first step in meeting any challenge is always an intelligent and informed citizenry. The purpose of this series is to educate our readers so that they can make informed decisions about issues related to drugs and drug abuse.

SUGGESTED ADDITIONAL READING

Courtwright, David T. *Forces of Habit, Drugs and the Making of the Modern World.* Cambridge, Mass: Harvard University Press, 2001. David T. Courtwright is Professor of History at the University of North Florida.

Davenport-Hines, Richard. *The Pursuit of Oblivion, A Global History of Narcotics.* New York: Norton, 2002. The author is a professional historian and a member of the Royal Historical Society.

Huxley, Aldous. *Brave New World.* New York: Harper & Rowe, 1932. Huxley's book, written in 1932, paints a picture of a cloned society devoted only to the pursuit of happiness.

David J. Triggle, Ph.D.
University Professor
School of Pharmacy and Pharmaceutical Sciences
State University of New York at Buffalo

1

Prescription Drug Abuse and Misuse: A Global Perspective

Drug abuse is an enormous problem among adolescents today. Overall, teenage drug abuse and teenage abuse of substances such as marijuana, alcohol, and tobacco has declined in recent years, but the abuse of prescription drugs, such as barbiturates, by teenagers has been steadily increasing. This has led authorities to label the current teen generation "Generation Rx."[1]

The National Institute on Drug Abuse conducts a survey every year called "Monitoring the Future." This survey polls eighth, tenth,

NO CURE FOR ANXIETY

Nicolette started taking Xanax when she was in eighth grade. Her parents were getting a divorce, and each day felt worse than the previous one. She couldn't believe that her dad had left, and she was really worried about her mom, who spent every night crying in the family room. In her mom's medicine cabinet, Nicolette found some pills, called alprazolam or Xanax, which were for anxiety. She thought if they were helping her mom, they would probably be good for her, too. Nicolette took the pills, and she felt more relaxed and was able to sleep at night without worrying. She began taking more and more of the pills; and because her mother was so caught up in other things, she never even noticed.

Nicolette's teacher noticed a change in Nicolette, though. She was falling asleep in class and not completing her assignments. She also stopped worrying about how she looked and came to school with dirty clothes and messy hair. The teacher voiced her concerns to Nicolette's mom, and although she didn't believe her daughter could be on drugs, she followed the teacher's advice and locked the medicine cabinet. Nicolette couldn't get to the Xanax. Within a day, her mind was racing and she was in a panic. She missed school because she felt so terrible. Her mom came home from work and found her thrashing on her bedroom floor. She was having a seizure. Thankfully, Nicolette's mom got her to the hospital in time to get her appropriate care. Nicolette spent the next month living at a hospital being treated for drug addiction to and physical dependence on Xanax.

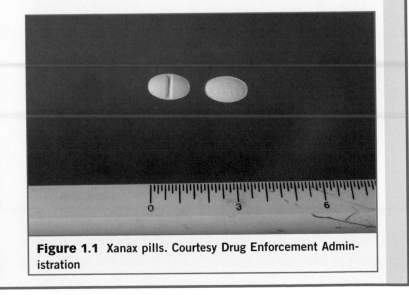

Figure 1.1 Xanax pills. Courtesy Drug Enforcement Administration

Table 1.1 **Monitoring the Future Study: Trends in Prevalence of Various Drugs for 8th Graders, 10th Graders, and 12th Graders**

8TH GRADERS	2001	2002	2003	2004
Lifetime	26.8	24.5	22.0	21.5
Annual	119.5	17.7	16.1	15.2
30-day	11.7	10.4	9.7	8.4
10TH GRADERS	2001	2002	2003	2004
Lifetime	45.6	44.6	41.4	39.8
Annual	37.2	34.8	32.0	31.14
30-day	22.7	20.8	19.5	18.3
12TH GRADERS	2001	2002	2003	2004
Lifetime	53.9	52.0	51.1	51.1
Annual	1.4	41.0	39.3	38.8
30-day	25.7	25.4	24.1	23.4

Source: National Institute on Drug Abuse

and twelfth graders on their views and experience with drug use. Data for 2004 showed that overall illicit drug abuse had decreased among teens that year (Table 1.1) compared to previous years. However, other surveys indicated a rise in teenage abuse of prescription drugs.[2]

The 2004 Partnership Attitude Tracking Study (PATS), conducted by Partnership for a Drug-Free America, showed that prescription drug abuse is higher than or on par with most other illicit substances (Figure 1.2). PATS data indicates that one in five teenagers has abused **Vicodin®**, and one in ten has abused **OxyContin®** (a pain medication) or a stimulant such as **Ritalin®** (a medication to control **attention-deficit/hyperactivity disorder**, or ADHD).

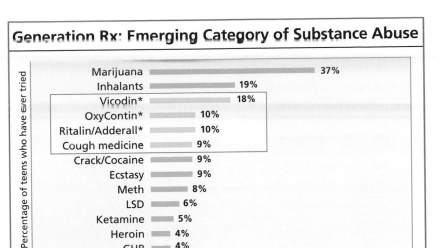

Figure 1.2 Abuse of prescription drugs has become part of teen culture. After marijuana and inhalants, more teens have tried prescription drugs than any other class of drugs. Source: Partnership for a Drug-Free America

Prescription drug abuse has infiltrated current teen culture. PATS data revealed that 37 percent of teens say they have close friends who have abused prescription painkillers like Vicodin and OxyContin. Some 29 percent say the same about prescription stimulants Ritalin and **Adderall®**. Average teens demonstrate a remarkable sophistication and knowledge when it comes to prescription (Rx) medications, which must be subscribed and supervised by a doctor, over-the-counter (OTC) medications, which are available for general purchase and use, and all other drugs. Teens are familiar with brand names of a wide variety of medications and can accurately describe their effects.

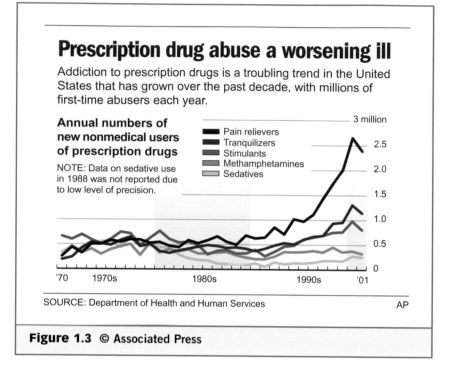

Prescription drug abuse a worsening ill

Addiction to prescription drugs is a troubling trend in the United States that has grown over the past decade, with millions of first-time abusers each year.

Annual numbers of new nonmedical users of prescription drugs

NOTE: Data on sedative use in 1988 was not reported due to low level of precision.

- Pain relievers
- Tranquilizers
- Stimulants
- Methamphetamines
- Sedatives

3 million
2.5
2.0
1.5
1.0
0.5
0

'70   1970s   1980s   1990s   '01

SOURCE: Department of Health and Human Services   AP

Figure 1.3 © Associated Press

DRUG ABUSE TERMS

Abuse of **psychoactive substances** (those that affect the mind or mental processes) is difficult to specifically define. The American Psychiatric Association (APA) published the fourth edition of the *Diagnostic and Statistical Manual of Mental Disorders*, or *DSM–IV*. The APA defines criteria related to mental disorders as a whole, including drug abuse, in technical language used mainly for research purposes.[3] Health care professionals have attempted to simplify these definitions for use in everyday practice. With regard to psychoactive substances, the first distinction must be made between drug use and drug abuse. The following definitions have been suggested:

Prescription drug use: The use of a medication in a socially accepted manner, which is recommended by a doctor or healthcare professional, to control mood or state of mind. An example of use would be a patient taking a medication prescribed by their doctor to calm their anxiety. The medication does affect their mind and body, but they are using it in a recommended, safe manner.[4]

Prescription drug abuse (or problematic use): The use of a medication to change or control state of mind in an illegal manner or a manner that is harmful to one's self. An example of this is a person stealing his or her family member's medication and taking that drug to get high. Substance abuse is dangerous because even safe medications may be dangerous when used inappropriately.

With regard to prescription drug use, it is also important to define the difference between *drug addiction* and *physical dependence* so that we may appropriately identify drug abuse and addiction. This helps prevent confusion with appropriate drug use, which over time may lead to physical dependence.

Drug addiction: Repeated, compulsive seeking or use of a drug despite bad physical, social, or psychological consequences of use. People with drug addictions will continue using a drug even though they do not require it to treat a medical condition. An example of drug addiction is a person who continues abusing a drug to get high even though they have missed days of school or had a car accident as a result.

Physical dependence: Physical dependence occurs when a person's body becomes accustomed to a certain medication and cannot function properly without it. Only certain medications can cause physical dependence. Individuals who are physically dependent on a medication cannot discontinue that drug suddenly, but instead must be slowly weaned off of the medication. If the medication is stopped abruptly, patients will experience physical symptoms of withdrawal and may become very ill.

Individuals who are physically dependent on a medication are not necessarily addicts. The distinction occurs because individuals who are only physically dependent will choose to discontinue a medication when they no longer require it to treat a medical condition. Addicts will continue to take the medication to get high with no intention of stopping. An example of physical dependence is a cancer patient who requires large doses of pain medication and who would experience a withdrawal syndrome if that medication was stopped. Such a patient would not seek this medication, however, if they no longer experienced pain, and so their dependency does not make them a drug addict.

Drug addicts may become physically dependent on the drugs that they abuse, but this is not always the case because some drugs of abuse will not cause physical dependence, although it is possible to become psychologically dependent on them. Either way, addicts seek a medication to get high, not to treat a medical condition.

COMMONLY ABUSED PRESCRIPTION DRUGS

Not all prescription drugs have the potential to be abused. Prescription drugs that have abuse potential are regulated by government agencies including the Drug Enforcement Agency (DEA) under the *Controlled Substances Act (CSA)*. The CSA places all substances regulated under existing federal law into one of five schedules based upon the substance's medicinal value, harmfulness, and potential for abuse or addiction. Schedule I is reserved for the most dangerous drugs that have no recognized medical use, while Schedule V is the classification used for the least dangerous drugs. The act also provides a mechanism for substances to become controlled, added to a schedule, decontrolled, removed from control, or rescheduled.[5]

There are three major classes of prescription drugs of abuse: **opioids**, **central nervous system (CNS) depressants**, and **stimulants**. Opioids are medications often prescribed to treat pain. They work on special parts of the brain to relieve

Table 1.2 Examples of Commonly Abused Prescription Medications

Opioids	Morphine Hydromorphone (Dilaudid) Meperidine (Demerol) Methadone Fentanyl Propoxyphene (Darvocet) Hydrocodone (Vicodin) Oxycodone (OxyContin, Percocet)
CNS Depressants	Benzodiazepines (lorazepam [Ativan]), alprazolam (Xanax), diazepam (Valium) Barbiturates (phenobarbital, secobarbital, pentobarbital)
Stimulants	Amphetamine Methylphenidate (Ritalin)

pain, and they cause a good feeling that may lead to abuse. CNS depressants, such as tranquilizers and sedatives, are often used to treat anxiety and sleep disorders by slowing normal brain function. The two main classes of depressants are **barbiturates** and **benzodiazepines**. Stimulants are prescribed to treat **narcolepsy**, a condition where people fall asleep unexpectedly, and attention-deficit/hyperactivity disorder. They increase alertness, attention, and energy, which are accompanied by increases in blood pressure, heart rate, and respiration. With a prescription from a doctor or health care professional, all of these medications may be safely used to treat various medical conditions, but they are all dangerous when abused.[6]

CAUSES OF PRESCRIPTION DRUG ABUSE

There are many reasons why a teenager may choose to abuse prescription drugs. It may start because an individual is seeking relief from emotional stress or is encouraged to abuse drugs by peers. Individuals stressed over family or marital issues, depression or mental disorders, or a traumatic life experience may turn to drug abuse for relief. Addiction often develops because an individual feels better when he or she is high and receives positive reinforcement through drug abuse. Once an individual begins abusing a medication, it can be difficult to stop because he or she may become addicted to the feeling and/or become physically dependent on the substance (if it is a medication with that potential).

Persons between the ages of 18 and 25 are most likely to abuse illicit drugs. The younger a person is when they begin abusing alcohol and illicit drugs, the more likely they are to be a drug abuser later in life, especially if that abuse begins before age 15. Typically, the teenager whose drug involvement progresses to substance abuse begins with commercially available drugs such as alcohol and tobacco, progresses to marijuana abuse, and then goes on to using other drugs or different drug combinations. For this reason, alcohol, tobacco, and marijuana are often called "**gateway drugs**" because they "open the gate" to the abuse of other substances.

REASONS FOR INCREASE IN PRESCRIPTION DRUG ABUSE

Why is prescription drug abuse on the rise in teenagers today? One reason may be that the campaigns to inform teens of the dangers of **"street" drugs** have been so effective that they are turning to prescription drugs as an assumed safer alternative. PATS revealed that close to half of all teens incorrectly believe using prescription medications to get high is "much safer" than using street drugs. Close to one third also have the misconception that prescription painkillers are not addictive.

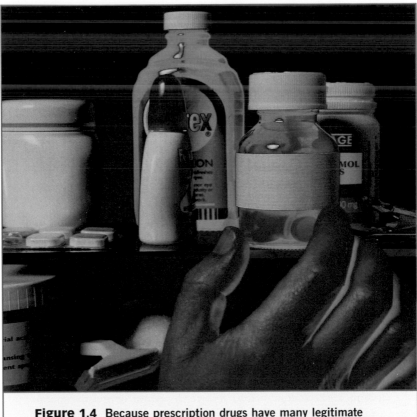

Figure 1.4 Because prescription drugs have many legitimate uses, they are often present in households, giving teens easy access to them. © M. Kulyk and V. de Schwanber/Photo Researchers, Inc.

Teens also cited "ease of access" of prescription medications as a major factor. Specifically, the majority stated that parents' medicine cabinets, and/or medicine cabinets in the homes of friends, are major access points. Some individuals obtain prescription drugs for abuse by "doctor shopping," by which the individuals continually switch physicians to get new prescriptions so that they can obtain enough medication to feed their addiction. Individuals may also illegally purchase medications from legitimate patients who require the drug for a medical condition. This has become common among teenagers who require Ritalin or Adderall for attention-deficit disorder, some of whom sell these medications to friends and classmates for the purpose of getting high.

RISKS OF PRESCRIPTION DRUG ABUSE

Abuse of drugs (including alcohol and tobacco) is the number-one cause of preventable illness and death in the United States. Each year, more than 500,00 deaths (or over one in four), in the United States are attributable to abuse of alcohol, tobacco, or other drugs. [7]

Prescription medications are safe when used appropriately, and under the supervision of a doctor, to treat a medical condition. However, abusing prescription medications is never safe and may lead to disastrous consequences. A medication beneficial to one person may cause a bad reaction in another, especially if that person is allergic or has a medical condition that can be worsened by the medication. Also, an appropriate dose of a medication for one person may not be appropriate for another, and may lead to overdose and sometimes fatal effects.

All prescription drug abuse may lead to harmful consequences such as accidents, injuries, blackouts, legal problems, and unsafe sexual behavior, which can increase the risk of acquiring sexually transmitted diseases (STDs) and human immunodeficiency virus (HIV). Specifically, each class of drugs has certain potentially life-threatening consequences of abuse. The abuse of opioids may lead to severe respiratory depression and inability to breathe, which can lead to death. Depressants may also cause respiratory depression and may lead to seizures if an addict suddenly stops taking them. Stimulants speed up the body's activities and raise blood pressure and heart rate, and when abused, may lead to a heart attack, stroke, or a seizure. Combinations of these drugs can increase the risks of a variety of life-threatening effects.[6]

WHAT CAN YOU DO TO STOP PRESCRIPTION DRUG ABUSE?

The first thing to do is educate yourself about the dangers of drug abuse. This book will teach you about the effects associated with one class of drugs of abuse, the barbiturates. In the following chapters you will learn what the barbiturates are and their current legal and illegal uses. Most importantly, you will learn about one of the first steps in combating

LETHAL COMBINATION

Aiden had just begun high school and felt really cool because some of the seniors had invited him to a party that none of the other underclassmen had been invited to attend. One of the seniors, Tom, said his parents had gone out of town and he had the whole house to himself. At the party, the seniors were all taking OxyContin (an opioid), which one of the seniors had stolen from his dad's pharmacy. Aiden decided to take a couple of pills with some of the other guys. They said it was fine and that they did it all the time. Aiden felt so relaxed from the pills that he found it easy to talk to the girl he liked, Katie, even though he was usually too nervous to even say "Hi" to her. Katie asked Aiden if he wanted to have some beer with her, and they had a few drinks.

About an hour later Aiden felt so tired he laid down on the couch to take a nap. Katie covered him with a blanket and left. Aiden never woke up. The combination of OxyContin and beer had been strong enough to stop Aiden's breathing. Tom found him dead on the couch the next morning.

barbiturate abuse, which is through the identification of an abuser and treatment of abuse. It is also important to understand the legal consequences of drug abuse. With all of this knowledge, you and those around you will understand the impact of abuse of barbiturates and other prescription drugs and how you can stop it.

2

Effect of Barbiturates on the Body

Barbiturates depress, or slow down and weaken, the body's activities. Barbiturates' effects are stronger in the brain than the rest of the body. Higher and higher doses of barbiturates would slow the brain's functions more and more, while the rest of the body, including muscles and other organs like the heart, would only be affected by very high doses.[9,10,11]

In small doses, barbiturates mildly depress brain functions. They initially cause a feeling of excitement, confusion, and **euphoria** (a feeling of great happiness and well-being). This initial high entices people to abuse these agents, although the feeling is quickly followed by sleepiness and sedation. Elderly people and very young children may actually experience a paradoxical, or opposite, effect and become energetic and nervous after taking barbiturates.

Higher doses of barbiturates lead to more significant depression of brain function, with effects similar to those of alcohol intoxication. Individuals may experience impaired judgement, slurred speech, and poor coordination. The part of the brain that controls these functions becomes affected, making them unsteady and unsafe to operate a motor vehicle. Even higher doses of barbiturates may cause a person to pass out or fall asleep.

Barbiturates effects generally last only a few hours, how-ever they may produce a hangover effect the day after con-sumption, leaving the individual depressed, angry, and with poor judgement. They may also have trouble with coordina-tion and still be unable to safely operate a motor vehicle.

In even higher doses barbiturates can be life threatening, unless administered in a hospital under the supervision of a doctor. Very high doses of barbiturates can cause different body systems to shut down. The biggest danger is their effect on the part of the brain that controls respiration, because high doses can depress it so much that a person stops breathing. Very high doses also begin to depress other organs, such as the heart, which may be left unable to supply the brain and body with oxygen and nutrient-rich blood. High doses may also stop peristalsis, or movement of food through the gastrointestinal tract, which can cause constipation and eventually poisoning if the body is unable to expel toxic substances through a bowel movement.

HOW DO DOCTORS DETERMINE THE DIFFERENCE BETWEEN SAFE AND UNSAFE DOSES OF BARBITURATES?

All barbiturates currently available cause a continuum of depression of body function, from sleepiness to shutting down of necessary functions. The amount of depression or weakening is increased by many factors, the most obvious being dose. The more barbiturates a person takes, the greater depression will occur. Barbiturates are considered "**narrow therapeutic index drugs**." This means there is a very small difference between an effective and a lethal dose of barbiturates.

Two other factors that increase depression are more potent formulations, and injecting barbiturates rather than taking them by mouth. Different formulations of barbiturates are available (as discussed in Chapter 4), and some of these for-mulations are more potent, or stronger, than others. Therefore if two people took the same dose of two different barbiturates, the person taking the more potent agent would be more affected than the person taking the weaker formulation. Agents that are injected have larger effects because more of the drug reaches the bloodstream and brain to exert its effects. When agents are ingested some of the drug is destroyed in the stomach before it gets to the bloodstream.

Barbiturates may exert stronger depressant effects in people based on their age, physical and emotional state, and other medications they may be taking. Other depressants, such as sleeping pills or alcohol, will greatly increase the effects of barbiturates when taken together. Therefore, a barbiturate dose that may make one person slightly tired could put another person to sleep and cause them to stop breathing. This is why it is very important to only use these medications under the careful direction of a doctor or other knowledgeable health care provider. If a doctor is going to prescribe a barbiturate, he or she will consider all of these variables when choosing a formulation and dose. There is no way for a person who is not a trained professional to predict the effects that a certain barbiturate drug and dose are going to have on a specific person. There is no way to know if a dose may or may not lead to an accidental, life-threatening overdose without the expertise of a physician.

Individuals who take barbiturates regularly may develop tolerance to their effects, which means that patients may need higher doses to achieve the same medicinal effects and addicts may require higher doses to achieve the same initial high. The effect of barbiturates may be weaker in a person who is tolerant versus a person who is naive, meaning they have never taken the drug before. People who take barbiturates must be cautious, because although their tolerance will require them to take higher doses to achieve the same depressant effects, the amount of drug required to cause a fatal overdose will barely change. Therefore regular users of

DANGEROUS PARTYING

Samantha was in her freshman year of high school and had decided to throw a party at her house while her parents were out of town for the weekend. Samantha invited everyone, including upperclassmen, to her house on Saturday night. Some of the upperclassmen brought a keg of beer, and everyone was drinking and dancing.

One of Samantha's friends found some medication in the bathroom medicine cabinet. Samantha's mom suffered from migraine headaches and took a medication, Fioricet®, which contains the barbiturate butalbital. Samantha's friend told everyone they could get high from it. Samantha assumed it was perfectly safe as she had seen her mother take two of these pills at a time to relieve her migraines, without any bad side effects. Samantha and several of her friends took two pills each, and everyone felt an awesome high. Later in the evening everyone began passing out all over Samantha's house. Samantha felt sleepy but decided to check on her friend Sarah, who had taken some Fioricet along with her beer and was acting especially drunk. Sarah was lying unconscious in the corner. Samantha looked closer and saw she wasn't breathing.

Samantha panicked and ran next door to get her neighbor, who began to perform CPR on Sarah. She then called 911, and when the ambulance came, paramedics put a breathing tube down Sarah's throat and gave her life-saving medications. Sarah spent three days in the hospital recovering. If Samantha had not found her at just that moment, Sarah would never have woken up. The doctors explained that some people, like Sarah, have a stronger reaction to barbiturates than others. The alcohol Sarah consumed also had depressant properties and contributed to stopping her breathing.

barbiturates must follow their doctor's instructions very carefully. As these patients build a tolerance and require higher doses of barbiturates, the risk of an accidental, deadly overdose becomes more likely.

HOW BARBITURATES WORK IN THE BRAIN

It is not completely understood how barbiturates work, although doctors believe barbiturates activate receptors in the brain, called **GABA receptors**. GABA receptors are messengers in the brain and nervous system that tell different body functions to slow down when they are activated. Barbiturates activate GABA receptors that produce depressant effects, meaning they tell different brain functions to slow down. All barbiturates are depressants, meaning they depress the body's functions, especially brain functions. Barbiturates also possess **anticonvulsant** properties, meaning they can prevent seizures in people who are prone to this condition.

ADDICTIVE POTENTIAL OF BARBITURATES

Barbiturates are addictive and have the potential to be abused. Individuals abuse barbiturates to gain an initial high followed by a drunk feeling similar to that obtained with alcohol use. In 2001, 8.7 percent of high school seniors admitted they had tried barbiturates to get high. Abusers of barbiturates have a high risk of accidental overdose. This overdose may lead to shutting down of necessary organs in the body, such as the heart, and may lead a person to stop breathing. This may be fatal.

DRUG-DRUG INTERACTIONS WITH BARBITURATES

Use of barbiturates combined with many other medications has been reported to alter the effects of barbiturates or the other drugs. Most of these drug interactions have been specifically reported with the barbiturate **phenobarbital**. There are

GABA and the Chloride Channel

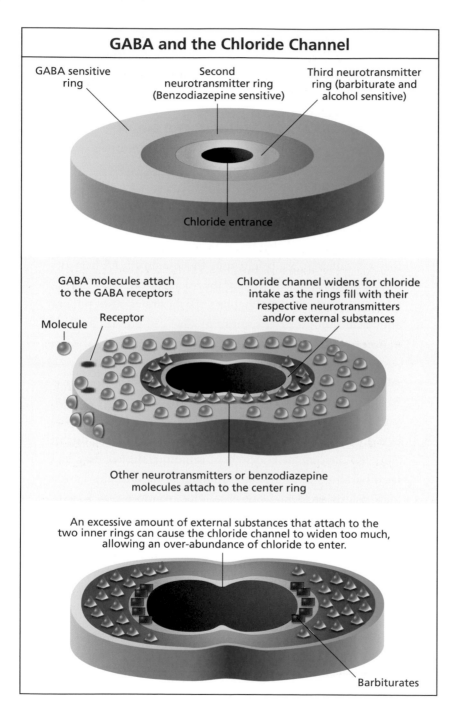

GABA sensitive ring

Second neurotransmitter ring (Benzodiazepine sensitive)

Third neurotransmitter ring (barbiturate and alcohol sensitive)

Chloride entrance

GABA molecules attach to the GABA receptors

Chloride channel widens for chloride intake as the rings fill with their respective neurotransmitters and/or external substances

Molecule   Receptor

Other neurotransmitters or benzodiazepine molecules attach to the center ring

An excessive amount of external substances that attach to the two inner rings can cause the chloride channel to widen too much, allowing an over-abundance of chloride to enter.

Barbiturates

two main ways barbiturates may interact with other medications, including additive side effects and by affecting the liver, which may change how the body processes and uses certain medications. Medications with depressant effects such as alcohol, tranquilizers, antihistamines, and other sedatives may increase the depressive side effects of barbiturates. When barbiturates interact with other drugs by increasing the speed with which the liver processes and eliminates other medicines, the result can decrease the effectiveness of certain medications, such as **corticosteroids** (sometimes prescribed to treat severe asthma) and **doxycycline** (an antibiotic used to treat gum disease). Patients should always consult their doctor or pharmacist about potential drug interactions before starting a new medication while on a barbiturate.

EFFECTS OF BARBITURATES ON THE FETUS IN PREGNANT WOMEN

In pregnant women, the placenta is the tissue that connects the mother and fetus, or unborn child, to transport nourishment and take away waste. Barbiturates easily travel across the placenta. Therefore, pregnant women who take barbiturates are also giving roughly the same doses of the drugs to

Figure 2.1 (left) When activated, GABA receptors cause body functions to slow down (*top*). As indicated here, they are receptive to alcohol, barbiturates, and benzodiazipenes. GABA molecules attach to the receptors (*middle*), causing the chloride channel to widen. Chloride neutralizes norepinephrine and has a calming affect. When the chloride channel widens too much due to the action of external substances (*bottom*), an excess of chloride enters and can cause the body to slow down too much. © 2005 Neurogenesis, Inc.; Concept by Dr. Terry Neher, CCDS, CAC; Graphics by CedarCanyonMarketing.com

Figure 2.2 Blood flows through a human placenta to reach fetal tissue, and the baby. © John Bavosi/Photo Researchers, Inc.

their unborn babies. Babies exposed to barbiturates **in utero**, or while being carried in their mother's uterus, may experience many bad side effects. Pregnant women who take barbiturates have a much higher risk of having children with birth defects, such as bleeding disorders, smaller head circumferences, problems with cognition, and other malformations. Within the first day of life, babies born to women who consumed barbiturates may experience life-threatening internal bleeding as a side-effect of barbiturate exposure. Babies of mothers who consumed barbiturates while pregnant may also experience a withdrawal syndrome within a few weeks of birth. Withdrawal symptoms could include extreme irritability and seizures. Women should never consume barbiturates while pregnant, unless they have a serious medical condition that can only be treated with barbiturates. Only in this rare instance may a woman, with advice from her doctor, accept the risk to her baby in order to protect her own health.

Barbiturates are also present in high concentrations in the breast milk of women who take them. Infants who consume this breast milk may experience side effects like excess sleepiness and lethargy. They may also experience withdrawal symptoms when weaned from breast milk. Long-term adverse effects of infant exposure to barbiturates in breast milk have not been well documented. However, the American Academy of Pediatrics cautions against breast-feeding while taking barbiturates because there may be risks to the infant.

3

History of Medical Uses of Barbiturates

The German scientist Adolf von Baeyer developed **barbituric acid** in a laboratory in 1863. Baeyer combined **urea**, a substance taken from animal urine, with **malonic acid**, a type of acid that comes from fruit, to produce barbituric acid. His development came on December 4, the day of the celebration of Saint Barbara, so Baeyer combined "Barbara" with "urea" to coin the name "barbiturates." Since his discovery, more than 2,000 different barbiturate compounds have been developed in laboratories, about 50 of which have been used as medicine for humans at some time in history.[12]

CHEMICAL STRUCTURE

A chemical structure is a diagram showing the microscopic arrangement of atoms within a molecule. Scientists use this blueprint to understand what ingredients are contained in and used to make a certain formulation. Barbiturates all contain the core chemical structure of barbituric acid, which by itself does not exert medicinal effects in the body. By adding or replacing different elements in barbituric acid, scientists can cause different barbiturate formulations to exert different effects in the body. Scientists may change the molecule so barbiturates have stronger or weaker depressant effects on the body, or to increase or decrease the duration of a formulation's effects. Scientists may also change the way a barbiturate is absorbed so it can be given orally, as a pill, rather than intravenously.[13]

Figure 3.1 Johann Friedrich Wilhelm Adolf von Baeyer.
© Edgar Fahs Smith Collection, University of Pennsylvania Library

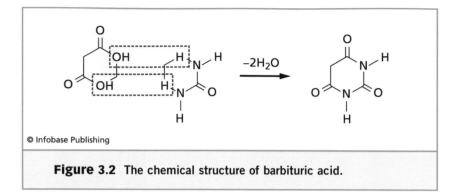

Figure 3.2 The chemical structure of barbituric acid.

HISTORY OF MEDICAL USE

The researchers Joseph von Mering and Emil Fischer, a student of von Baeyer, developed the first barbiturate drug to be marketed. Fischer produced 5.5-diethylbarbituric acid, a **hypnotic** (medication to help patients sleep) and **sedative** (medication to relax people with constant nervousness and anxiety). This sedative/hypnotic drug was known by the trade names **Barbital**, **Veronal**, and **Dorminal**. Barbital proved to be a more effective sedative/hypnotic agent and replaced the class of drugs, sedative bromides, which were used at the time. [14]

By 1912, von Mering and Fischer developed and commercially introduced a new barbiturate compound for sleep and anxiety called phenobarbital or Luminal. However, this medication quickly found its place as treatment for a very different medical condition, **epilepsy**, which is a condition of periodic, unprovoked convulsions or seizures. The main goal of epilepsy treatment is to decrease the frequency of seizures. Alfred Hauptmann discovered the anti-epileptic properties of phenobarbital accidentally. A 1912 report by Hauptmann described epileptic patients who were given phenobarbital for sedation and incidentally had fewer seizures. Seizures are caused by an abnormal impulse in the brain, which spreads and sends inappropriate message to the body. These messages result in

Figure 3.3 Nobel Prize winning chemist Emil Fischer at work in his laboratory. © Corbis

seizures. Phenobarbital works by slowing down these abnormal impulses. At the time of Hauptmann's discovery there were very few treatment options available for patients with epilepsy,

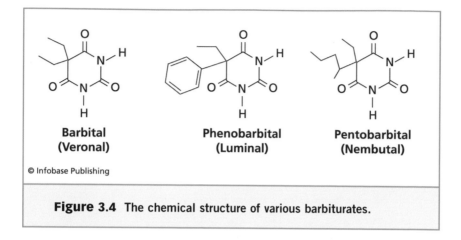

Barbital
(Veronal)

Phenobarbital
(Luminal)

Pentobarbital
(Nembutal)

© Infobase Publishing

Figure 3.4 The chemical structure of various barbiturates.

and so phenobarbital was marketed for this purpose and became widely used.

There have been more than 2,000 barbiturate derivatives developed from Baeyer's original formula. Barbiturates had so many uses initially that they were termed "wonder drugs," but in the 1960s their medical uses began to decline due to terrible side effects, risk of overdose, addictive potential, and development of newer, effective replacement medications with fewer side effects. Barbiturates side effects include: sleepiness, dizziness, nausea, impaired memory, impaired judgement, lack of motivation, **impotence** (inability of a man to have an erection), reduced sex drive, and breathing disorders. Barbiturates also have a high risk of accidental overdose, especially with regular use, because the difference between an effective dose and a lethal dose is very small and regular users develop a tolerance that requires higher doses to obtain the same medical benefits. While possible overdose is a serious concern under a doctor's care, the risk only increases among people who abuse the drug. Finally, although barbiturates are effective, their risks led scientists to develop other safer drugs to replace them.

Benzodiazepines are one class of drugs that largely replaced barbiturates for many indications. These drugs are as

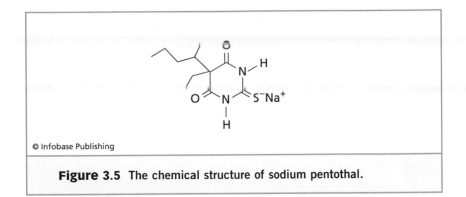

© Infobase Publishing

Figure 3.5 The chemical structure of sodium pentothal.

effective as barbiturates, but have far fewer side effects and a lower risk of overdose.

Another significant event in the history of barbiturates was the *Controlled Substances Act of 1970*, created by the United States government to restrict use of potential drugs of abuse. This act divided regulated drugs into five schedules that govern the legal distribution and use of most drugs with a significant abuse potential. The Drug Enforcement Administration (DEA) is the primary federal agency responsible for enforcing these regulations to prevent drug abuse and for coordinating national and international efforts to reduce illicit drug supply. Therefore, this classification scheme is often referred to as the *DEA Schedules*. Schedule I substances have a high abuse liability and no approved medical use. These substances, such as heroin and marijuana, are available for investigational purposes only and are not approved for patient use. Pharmacies do not sell these compounds nor can physicians write prescriptions for them. Schedule II–IV substances have decreasing abuse liabilities (II is the highest) and approved medical uses. Physicians are licensed to prescribe these compounds, and pharmacies can dispense them, although pharmacies do not stock all of these substances. Schedule II compounds have more stringent record-keeping and storage requirements than do Schedule III and IV

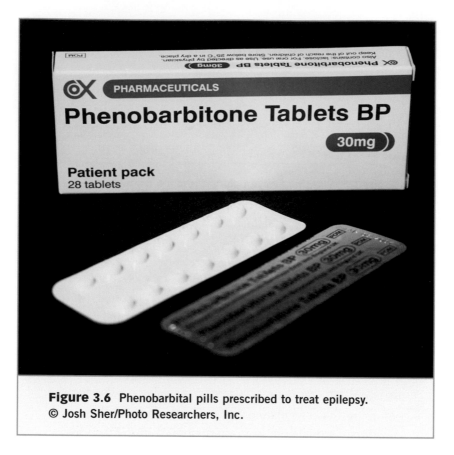

Figure 3.6 Phenobarbital pills prescribed to treat epilepsy.
© Josh Sher/Photo Researchers, Inc.

substances. Schedule V substances have the lowest abuse potential and are available without a prescription.

All barbiturates have the potential to be abused and cause addiction. Different barbiturates are designated as schedule II, III, and IV drugs, which means that all barbiturates require a prescription from a doctor or health care provider and the prescription must contain the doctor's DEA number. Physicians must obtain a special license to get a DEA number in order to prescribe controlled or addictive substances such as barbiturates. Doctors are very cautious about prescribing barbiturates to patients who have a history of drug abuse.

Pharmacists also take special precautions when dispensing controlled substances, to ensure they are used appropriately to treat medical conditions and not abused.

A+ THE PHARMACY

Jaina was diagnosed with a seizure condition known as epilepsy. Her doctor, Dr. Smith, prescribed a medication, phenobarbital, for her condition. He explained that phenobarbital is a controlled substance because it has the risk of being abused. Therefore, Dr. Smith used a special controlled substances prescription pad to write Jaina's prescription and included his DEA number on the prescription.

At the pharmacy the pharmacist, Lisa, called Dr. Smith to ensure that he actually wrote the prescription. Lisa does this before dispensing controlled substances to ensure the prescriptions are not fake. Sometimes addicts submit fake prescriptions that were not written by a qualified physician or health care provider to attempt to purchase controlled substances illegally. After Dr. Smith verified he had written the prescription, Lisa removed the phenobarbital from a locked cabinet and counted out Jaina's pills. These are some of the precautions pharmacists take when dispensing controlled substances, to prevent abusers from obtaining them illegally or stealing them from the pharmacy.

4

Current Medical Uses of Barbiturates

In the last hundred years barbiturates have been important drugs in the treatment of many serious medical conditions. While being effective for such conditions as epilepsy, though, barbiturates also have many negative side effects, including tiredness, dizziness, and risk of abuse and addiction. The worst side effect is the high risk of accidental overdose due to barbiturates' "narrow therapeutic index," which means the difference between an effective dose and a lethal overdose is very small.[15] Since all people are different and there are many factors that may affect a drug's action in a specific person, doctors must be very careful when setting or increasing the dose of a barbiturate drug, because a small dose increase may lead to an overdose. Many other types of drugs available now are much safer and often as effective as barbiturates for many medical conditions. Therefore, barbiturates are generally not a doctor's first choice for treatment anymore, though they are still used carefully in special cases. A doctor may choose a barbiturate when a person does not respond to newer drug therapies, or in combination with a newer drug when a patient needs an additional therapy for his or her condition. For some disease states, such as infantile seizures, barbiturates remain the first drug chosen for treatment, despite the risk of side effects, because they are the only drugs proven to be effective for that condition.

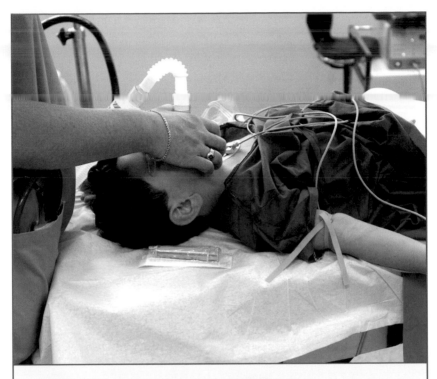

Figure 4.1 Doctors sometimes use barbiturates for general anesthesia during surgery. © Phanie/Photo Researchers, Inc.

CLASSIFICATION OF BARBITURATES

Several barbiturate compounds are on the market for various medical uses. Different barbiturates come as formulations that may be taken by mouth, per rectum, by injection into a muscle, or by injection into a vein (directly into the bloodstream). Most barbiturates are currently classified according to the duration of time they exert their effects in the body. They are divided into three categories: **long acting**, **intermediate-acting**, and **short-acting**. Long-acting barbiturates are best for conditions that require **chronic use**, meaning use on a regular basis, like epilepsy, because patients do not need to remember to take them as often.[16]

Some barbiturates are classified as general anesthetics because they are given intravenously to put people to sleep during surgery. These agents start working very quickly, within a minute, and are effective for a very short amount of time. This is beneficial because doctors can put people to sleep for surgery very quickly and can continue to administer these drugs until they want the patient to wake up. They can also wake the patients up within a few minutes after discontinuing drug administration, so the patient can begin recovery.

Finally barbiturates are found in combination products for **analgesia** or pain relief. The two most common are Fioricet and Fiorinal, although others exist.

Table 4.1 Barbiturate Products by Class[17]

Class	Generic Drug Name	Brand Name	Duration of Action
Long-Acting	mephobarbital	Mebaral	10–16 hours
	phenobarbital	Luminal	
	primidone	Mysoline	
Intermediate-Acting	amobarbital	Amytal	6–8 hours
	aprobarbital	Alurate	
	butabarbital	Butisol	
Short-Acting	pentobarbital	Nembutal	3–4 hours
	secobarbital	Seconal	
General Anesthetics	thiopental	Pentothal	<30 minutes
	methohexital	Brevita	
Combination Analgesics	acetaminophen/ caffeine and butalbital	Fioricet	Varies
	aspirin/caffeine and butalbital	Fiorinal	
	acetaminophen and butalbital		

CURRENT MEDICAL USES OF BARBITURATES
Sedative/Hypnotics

Barbiturates are still used as sedative/hypnotic agents (see Chapter 3), but they have been largely replaced by benzodiazepines for treatment of anxiety and insomnia (difficulty sleeping). Barbiturates are still used occasionally, but benzodiazepines have proven to be much safer and have less risk of accidental overdose.

Seizures

Barbiturates are still sometimes used for patients with seizure conditions, including epilepsy (see Chapter 3). Long-acting barbiturates, mephobarbital and phenobarbital, are still used to treat epilepsy in adults, who may take them every day to prevent seizures. Newer medications, though, have largely replaced barbiturates for treatment of epilepsy. Although barbiturates remain as effective as most newer epilepsy treatments, the newer drugs generally have far fewer side effects. They don't make people as tired, or impair their judgement and ability to drive and perform daily activities as much as barbiturates, and they have a much lower risk of life-threatening overdose. The newer drugs have a much larger buffer between a safe dose and poisonous dose, making it much more difficult to accidentally give a patient too much of these medicines. Therefore, because of safety concerns, barbiturates are mainly used today to treat epilepsy in adults who have tried and failed several newer therapies, and who find that barbiturates are the only effective agent. These patients must accept the bad side effects of barbiturates in order to get adequate treatment.[18]

Barbiturates are also used in infantile seizures that are not considered epilepsy. These seizures generally occur when an infant has a high fever, and therefore they are called **febrile seizures**. Phenobarbital is still commonly used to prevent seizures in infants, because scientists do not routinely study new drugs in infants and children. Because phenobarbital is such an old drug, doctors have gained experience through the years using it in children. They know that it is relatively safe and does not lead to any long-term consequences, like growth problems. Most infants outgrow their seizure condition and do not require lifelong medication.

Barbiturates may also be used to treat a life-threatening seizure condition called "**Status Epilepticus**." Most epileptic seizures last for several seconds and then resolve on their own, but occasionally a patient will continue seizing for several minutes or even hours. This can be very dangerous because the seizure may cause serious damage to the patient's muscles and internal organs. Patients with this condition must be admitted to a hospital, and injectable medicines must be used to try to stop the seizure. The first drugs that are tried are benzodiazepines and some newer anti-epileptic medications, but if these fail to break the seizure, barbiturates like pentobarbital or secobarbital are used.

Veterinary Medicine Uses

Barbiturates are used not only to treat human seizures. Phenobarbital is the most common medication used to treat seizures in pets, like dogs. Generally if pets have more than one seizure every one or two months they may need a medicine for seizure prevention, although a veterinarian should decide if one is necessary. Phenobarbital may be used alone or in combination with **potassium bromide**, a very old seizure medicine for humans. Like people, some young pets may grow out of their seizures as they mature.[19]

Diagnostic Testing

Two barbiturates, **methohexital** and **amobarbital**, are used for diagnostic purposes prior to brain surgery. This surgery is reserved for patients with very severe epilepsy, which does not respond to medications. Methohexital helps doctors find the place in an individual's brain that is causing the seizures, called

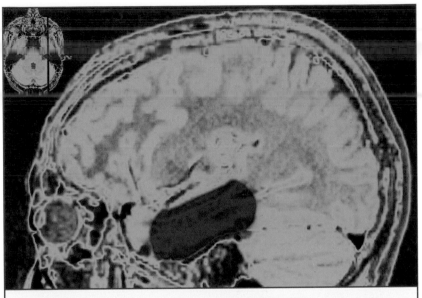

Figure 4.2 Magnetic resonance image (MRI) of the memory zone in the temporal lobe of the human brain. © James Cavallini/Photo Researchers, Inc.

the "**seizure focus**," so they know where to operate. This use was discovered in the late 1950s and has changed very little since that time. Amobarbital is used in a similar way to identify the part of an individual's brain that is most responsible for memory and language, prior to brain surgery.

Alcohol Withdrawal

Patients with mild symptoms of alcohol withdrawal do not generally require medication therapy. Benzodiazepines, like diazepam or alprazolam, are the treatment of choice for patients with severe alcohol withdrawal syndromes like "**delirium tremens**." Barbiturates can also be used for this disorder, but are often less prescribed because they are not as safe as benzodiazepines. Both barbiturates and benzodiazepines are effective in treating the anxiety, tremor, insomnia, and hand tremors associated with delirium tremens.

5

Illegal Use of Barbiturates

Many teens do not know what barbiturates are and what harmful effects may arise from abusing them. It is important to understand why barbiturates and other drugs are abused and to learn about the ultimate consequences of abuse.

REASONS WHY BARBITURATES ARE ABUSED

People abuse barbiturates for many reasons. Some teens may feel that they are cool or they fit in better because they abuse a drug. Some might think that drugs take their problems away without realizing that they simply mask them. This is Joey's issue, because he has problems at home. Also, a barbiturate may help to reduce anxiety. A quiet, introverted teen might become talkative and make friends more easily after taking a barbiturate.[20] Some people may think that using barbiturates will help others like them more. People who abuse stimulant drugs, such as Ritalin, might use a barbiturate to slow down after they use such a drug. Most addicts say that their motivation for drug use starts with seeking pleasure from taking the drug, and that they then continue using it for pleasure and to avoid the unpleasant effects of withdrawal.

HOW THESE DRUGS ARE ACQUIRED FOR ILLEGAL USE

Many parents and schoolteachers think their children and students can't get barbiturates or other drugs, but that is a misleading thought. It is simple enough to go online and type in "buy barbiturates" and get a list of different Web sites that sell prescription drugs without a prescription. "Buy prescriptions without a prescription," "barbiturate suppliers," and "cheap online pain relief and sleep aids" are taglines resulting from a simple search of the Internet. These illegal sites are part of the black market of drugs that makes these pills so easy to acquire. With a push of a button and a credit card, you can get a barbiturate delivered to your front door.[21]

It is also easy for someone to find a local seller of illegal drugs, such as marijuana, who can probably get other drugs,

JOEY'S STORY—PART I

Joey's parents were in the middle of a bitter and hateful divorce. Whenever they were in the house they yelled and screamed at each other. Forget about what happened when the two of them were in the same room. Joey did as much as he could to not be home. Thankfully he was 16 and could drive. He was able to go to friends' houses, sleep over many nights, and basically go anywhere to be away from the "mess" at home. After some time, Joey started to need other ways to get away from his parents and from reality.

On one of his trips he met a new guy who invited him to hang out with his friends. Joey thought these kids were cool. They drank and partied most nights, and it was easy for him to just hang out with them. He would drink, but he knew that he could get caught because his breath smelled. Getting pulled over for driving under the influence one time was all it would take for him to lose his license and his freedom from his parents. So, his friend gave him these pills that he called "red devils" or "blue heavens." Joey could get the same high he would from drinking alcohol, but even faster and without the smell of alcohol on his breath. He just didn't know what consequences would come from abusing these pills.

Figure 5.1 Online pharmacies fill prescriptions worldwide and some of them sometimes make illegal sales of controlled substances. © Andrew Holbrooke/Corbis

including barbiturates. What makes these products even more accessible is that most of them are available by prescription from a retail pharmacy. There have been cases when a pharmacy worker just took a bottle (or two or three, etc.) to sell or use illegally. Also, since barbiturates have legal uses, it's possible for a teen's parents to have them in their medicine cabinet, making access even easier.

SYMPTOMS OF DRUG ABUSE

Barbiturates at a dose used for proper medical treatment (seizure control or relief of pain from a migraine headache) cause their intended medical effect. In higher doses, they cause depression of the nervous system, which means that all bodily functions regulated by the nervous system, such as breathing and alertness, decrease. As the dose is increased, the effect of slowing down of the nervous system occurs to an even greater extent.[22] Barbiturate abuse has many negative effects, some of which occur from crossover with other drugs of abuse. It's important to realize that many of the signs of barbiturate abuse are also signs of other drug abuse in general. Learning to distinguish the signs will help you recognize and identify an abuser.

There is a wide spectrum of effects of barbiturate abuse. The most common and easiest to identify signs are slurred speech and confusion. A teen may look and act drunk, without the odor of alcohol on his or her breath. A major sign is lying, such as making up excuses for being late or covering up who they were hanging out with. A drug abuser might have bad mood swings, feeling happy one minute and depressed the next. Other signs include

- A sense of euphoria (that everything is fine and they are invincible)

- Bizarre behavior

- Paranoid thoughts (believing that someone or something is out to get them)

- Suicidal thoughts

- Combativeness

- Poor personal hygiene (not showering, not washing their hair or clothes)[23]

Another sign of drug abuse is being uninhibited or having what is called an **exaggerated personality**. This can be seen when someone who is very shy becomes very outgoing or obnoxiously loud when under the influence. He or she might act on sexual impulses they would normally suppress, because the abuser does not think clearly or understand the consequences of his or her actions. This can lead to unsafe sex, pregnancy, and the spread of sexually transmitted diseases.

Most barbiturates are not available in intravenous (IV) form, but if the abuser is able to inject the drug, the consequences of IV drug use may result. Abusers may catch an infection where they inject themselves, an infection of their blood (such as HIV) because of a dirty needle or one contaminated through sharing with other users, an air bubble that moves to their brain (an embolism, which usually results in death), pneumonia, or infection of the valves of the heart.

TOLERANCE

With time barbiturate abusers need higher and higher doses to get high. Tolerance to the effects of barbiturates happens fairly quickly. Most users find that after one to two weeks of regular use they need higher doses to get them through the day and to get high. The user develops tolerance to the effects of mood, sedation, and the calming action of barbiturates. Because barbiturates have a narrow therapeutic index, a very small increase in dose can equal a very large increase in the effect of the drug. This means that overdose can happen quite easily. Taking one extra pill can sometimes lead to an overdose.[24]

TOXIC AND OVERDOSE REACTIONS

The amount of overdose situations associated with barbiturates abuse has dropped as other drugs, such as Ecstasy, have become more popular, but a barbiturate overdose is still very serious, and death can result. The signs and diagnosis of barbiturate overdose are both physical and measurable. Doctors can diagnose overdose by completing a physical exam of the patient, as well as confirming the diagnosis with the use of blood tests. These two measures combined help to determine the presence of overdose. A blood test that shows drug levels in the blood does not help to determine the severity of the overdose. There are different factors that establish this. In long-time barbiturate abusers, high blood levels may not indicate how bad their overdose is, because their body can handle high doses.

JOEY'S STORY—PART II

Over the past two months Joey needed more and more of the pills to get high, and he needed to get high more often simply to get through each day. He stopped taking care of himself; he didn't shower or brush his teeth very often. He started lying to his teachers and his friends. He started stealing money from his mom or dad so he could keep buying the pills. His parents blamed each other for the missing money, and never considered that Joey was stealing it.

Joey slept, or more like passed out, for more than 10 hours during one of his drug binges. He just laid down flat on his back and lost consciousness. When he woke up, he could barely move. He found what looked like bruises on his back and the back of his legs, and on any part of his body that was down when he blacked out. They actually were not bruises but pools of blood that had formed because he had not moved for hours. Joey did not realize what he was doing to his body.

Some of the symptoms of a barbiturate or drug overdose include

- Impaired thinking

- Inability to follow simple instructions, such as touching one's nose

- Combative and resistant to medical help, perhaps fighting the doctor during a physical exam

When a toxic dose of barbiturates is taken, the patient becomes extremely sleepy (nearly comatose), has very shallow breathing, or may even stop breathing. He or she might have decreased (or no) response to painful stimuli (for example, not flinching when poked with a sharp pin) and loss of reflexes. The final outcome might be dangerously low blood pressure, which can lead to shock and, if not treated, to death.

TREATMENT OF BARBITURATE OVERDOSE

The most important way to treat a barbiturate overdose is through supportive care. Doctors monitor the patient's level of consciousness and vital signs. The patient can be given **activated charcoal,** a thick black substance that helps to block the absorption of the drug in the digestive tract. If the patient is in a coma or is not breathing, the first action is to put a breathing tube down his or her throat. They must be given fluids intravenously, as overdose victims are often dehydrated and have low blood pressure. Giving fluids will help to raise their blood pressure.

There is no drug or magic remedy that can help reverse the effects of barbiturates. For example, with an overdose of a narcotic, such as morphine, the drug **naloxone** can be given. With barbiturates, only time makes the overdose patient get better. Following overdose, the blood levels will go down and with this, the comatose state and the shallow breathing will lessen.

Figure 5.2 Capsules containing charcoal treated to increase its absorption capacity are used to absorb toxic substances. © GARO/PHANIE/Photo Researchers, Inc.

WITHDRAWAL OF BARBITURATES

Most addicts realize that they will suffer a great amount of pain and discomfort from barbiturate withdrawal if they stop taking the drug. The withdrawal of barbiturates for an addict can be extremely dangerous. Symptoms can range from tremors and irritability to seizures and death. Often, to help with the withdrawal symptoms, doctors prescribe another barbiturate, which is given in small and controlled doses. If the withdrawal is not done slowly, minor and major symptoms may develop over a short time.[25]

The first signs of withdrawal begin within 24 hours of discontinuing a barbiturate. Commonly, patients experience tremors, weakness, sweating, and restlessness. Patients may also get lightheaded and dizzy when moving from a recling or sitting position to a standing position. Tremors affect their entire body and are visible even when the person is resting. Often the tremors are severe enough to make tasks involving the hand

JOEY'S STORY—PART III

After six months of abusing barbiturates, Joey hit bottom. He was so depressed that he wanted to kill himself. One of his teachers was a former drug abuser, and he noticed Joey's erratic behavior, his sudden lack of interest in school, and realized he was abusing drugs. Mr. Wilson talked to Joey's parents, who finally started to pay attention to their son. After they confronted him, Joey broke down and told them everything. They entered Joey into an inpatient detox center. This was the best thing for him, although he felt like it was the worst. He got sick and threw up because he didn't have the pills anymore. He had terrible dreams and heard voices telling him, "You did this to yourself. You are the reason you are here and feel sick. It's your fault entirely." He was sick for seven days, and after the worst was over, he stayed in the hospital for a month. When he was released to home, he had sessions with a psychiatrist every few days. He has been clean for a year. He doesn't want to go through the withdrawal again; he plans on being clean for the rest of his life.

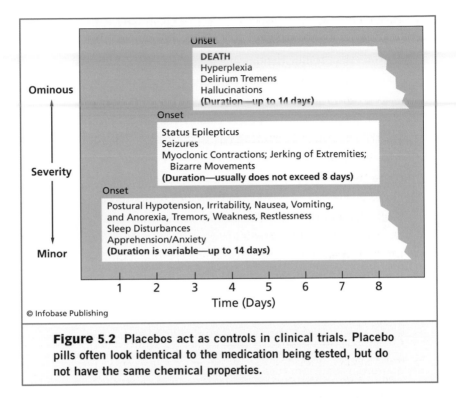

Onset

DEATH
Hyperplexia
Delirium Tremens
Hallucinations
(Duration—up to 14 days)

Ominous

Onset

Status Epilepticus
Seizures
Myoclonic Contractions; Jerking of Extremities;
    Bizarre Movements
(Duration—usually does not exceed 8 days)

Severity

Onset

Postural Hypotension, Irritability, Nausea, Vomiting,
and Anorexia, Tremors, Weakness, Restlessness
Sleep Disturbances
Apprehension/Anxiety
(Duration is variable—up to 14 days)

Minor

1   2   3   4   5   6   7   8
Time (Days)

© Infobase Publishing

Figure 5.2 Placebos act as controls in clinical trials. Placebo pills often look identical to the medication being tested, but do not have the same chemical properties.

(like holding a coffee cup) difficult to do. Additionally, patients may lose their appetites, feel nauseous, and vomit. When they are able to sleep, they might have very vivid dreams and nightmares. Their moods are not stable; they may feel anxious, perhaps paranoid about people around them. This anxiety can cause a fast heart rate and shortness of breath. These symptoms may last about a week.

When the patient has a more serious withdrawal, major symptoms may develop. The patient may have muscle contractions without thinking about them, and other bizarre patterns associated with movements can occur. This usually develops within 24 to 72 hours. It is during this time that the most serious consequence of withdrawal may be seen; the patient may have seizures, which at worst can take a long time to stop.

Hallucination: Between the third and eighth day hallucinations (seeing and hearing things that aren't there) and delirium may develop. Hallucinations due to barbiturate withdrawal are quite distinct. They are often auditory (meaning one hears voices) and occur while the person's mind is clear and he or she is seemingly alert. The voice is usually that of a third person (just like having someone else talk to them), and what it says is usually perverted. These hallucinations are almost identical to those seen with alcohol withdrawal. Alcohol is like a simpler chemical version of a barbiturate, so the connection can easily be made. Barbiturate use causes the same affects that alcohol use does and both cause a tired, dizzy reaction. It is very uncommon for a patient to experience visual hallucinations, but if they do occur, they are seen during the most serious parts of withdrawal and can last for a week, sometimes longer.

Delirium: Delirium due to barbiturate withdrawal is, again, similar to that seen with abrupt alcohol withdrawal. The chief sign is one of impaired memory, of both recent and past memories. Delirium is also associated with confusion and **disorientation** (not knowing person, place or time). The hallucinations associated with delirium are more visual in nature and are described as terrifying. Often, patients develop a high fever. These symptoms stop by the third or fourth day, and rarely last longer than a week.

Illegal use of barbiturates can lead to many serious consequences, and these drugs should never be considered safe, unless prescribed and monitored closely by a physician. Tolerance can easily develop, and a small increase in dose can lead to intoxication or overdose. The withdrawal effects of barbiturate abuse, like other drugs, are very unpleasant and can cause abusers to continue abusing for fear of feeling worse than ever before if they were to stop. With the help of treatment centers and doctors, however, abusers can overcome the symptoms of withdrawal and stay on the road to addiction recovery.

6

Identification and Prevention

WHY LOOK FOR DRUG ABUSE

There are a number of legal, safe uses for barbiturates, but they become a problem when a person misuses or abuses them habitually. First-time users can have severe, negative reactions, or even die, from barbiturates taken without a doctor's supervision. Regular abusers suffer from the long-term physical and psychological problems that make them unable to fully participate in society. Drug abuse affects not only users but also their families, friends, and everyone around them.

As a teen begins and continues to abuse drugs, his or her family can be affected in many ways. Addicts may lie and sneak around to keep their drug use secret from their family. They might stay out late and make up excuses for it. They might steal money from their mom's purses or their dad's wallets, and there may be times when they even steal money or other valuable possessions from siblings. The addicted teen may become hostile toward his or her family and set a bad example for younger siblings. On a whole, the addict can cause a great amount of trouble for everyone in the family and generate much hostility. Drug abuse can tear a family to pieces.[26,27]

The abuser may also have many social problems. Abuse can hurt friendships. Often abusers becomes enveloped in their new life hanging out with a new crowd, and thus they forget that their old friends even exist. They may act like they still like their old friends, but then start lying to and stealing from them. Overall, abusers become different people. Although they might fit in with their new friends, they usually alienate many others. Later when they are in recovery, their old friends may not support them anymore, having developed angry or hateful feelings toward their addiction and the drug.

Drug abuse also has many affects on society at large. According to the DEA more than 26,000 individuals died from drug-induced causes in the United States in 2002, and many more abused drugs.[28] Drug abuse can drive individuals to commit

IN WITH THE WRONG CROWD

Jen was a 14-year-old girl who seemed perfect in many ways. She was beautiful, received excellent grades, and was on the track team, captain of the varsity cheerleading club, and a member of numerous other clubs. At the beginning of school that year, she became friends with Mike, a senior in high school. Jen thought it was so cool that a senior wanted to hang out with her.

She started to spend a lot of time with Mike and his friends, and it was soon after this that Jen's mom noticed Jen's behavior change. She started getting home late. She was secretive about everything. One night she said she was going to sleep over at her best friend's house, and when Jen's mom called her friend's mom, Jen wasn't there. Jen came home the next morning, acting as if nothing was wrong, but her mom noticed a slight stumble in her walk. Over time Jen's grades fell, she got kicked off the cheerleading squad, and she lost interest in any activity related to school.

Jen's mom confronted her, and Jen finally broke down, saying that she felt a lot of pressure to be perfect all of the time. When she was with Mike and his friends, they didn't care about what she did, all because she took this medicine that made her feel good. With the pills around, she felt great, like she was on the top of her game.

crimes. They may steal money from stores, barbiturates from a pharmacy, or jewelry from homes so they can hock the valuables for money. Drugs often make a person irresponsible and dangerous to the people around them. People driving under the influence of a barbiturate might cause a car accident that kills themselves, their passengers, and innocent people in other vehicles.[29]

Drug use can also contribute to an increase in the number of diseases spread within a community. Someone high on drugs is more likely to have unsafe sex, leaving him or her exposed to herpes, chlamydia, human immunodeficiency virus (HIV), or other infections. Aside from the risk of disease, there is also the risk they might cause someone to become pregnant. If this is the case and their pregnant partner is a user, the baby might be born with a drug addiction.

There are two ways to calculate the costs of drug abuse on society. There are direct costs: drug treatment, healthcare costs, court fees, and lost wages. Indirect costs include: loss of productivity for those hurt in a drug-related crime, the pain and suffering abuse can cause, and drug-abuse related illness. Thus, the detection of drug abuse is not only important for the individual themselves, but for their family and friends, and for all of those around them.

IDENTIFICATION OF A DRUG ABUSER

Identifying a drug abuser is not an easy task, but there are a number of close people who can help to detect the signs. Family, friends, teachers, or doctors may realize that there is a problem with someone. It's also of great importance, however, for teens to have a good understanding of what to look for. Teens should learn not only how to identify barbiturate abusers, but also how to recognize people abusing any type of drug.

Friends often realize that someone is abusing drugs, even before it becomes apparent to a teen's family. There are a number of different indicators to look for, such as noticing that the person needs to use drugs to have a good time or cope with life, or seeing him or her hanging out with people who abuse the same drug or can buy it. Friends who break plans or are always late because they were getting high may also be abusing drugs. Other behaviors to be aware of include

- Coming to school high

- A friend losing interest in a certain activity (e.g., basketball) that he or she was always involved in

- Someone borrowing money to buy drugs or asking other people to hold his or her drugs

- Risky or unstable actions (such as having sex with a stranger or picking a fight with parents), causing friends to feel as if they must baby-sit when their friend is high

- A friend having difficulty with family relationships and letting his or her friends and family down

Family members may also notice if a child in their family is using drugs. Adults often find it hard to determine if a teen is using drugs, because teenagers are moody in general, have changes in their sleep patterns, and may often change hobbies. They think that their son's or daughter's strange behavior can be attributed to simply "being a teenager." After some time, though, a parent may begin to suspect drug use. A teen might have lower grades on their report card or miss school more often then they actually go. They may become very secretive about their possessions or activities or become abusive or violent. Their family might also notice that they are anxious or depressed, that they have a new group of friends, or that a prescription drug is now missing from the medicine cabinet. These changes may signal that something troubling involving a drug is going on.

A doctor may notice a number of signs or findings during a physical exam that signal a potential drug problem. The patient may suffer from depression, sleeping problems, or tremors. Other signs a doctor may notice are

- Frequent accidental injuries

- Digestive problems (e.g., stomach pain, diarrhea, constipation, or weight gain or loss)

- Sexual dysfunction

- An enlarged liver

- Changes in blood pressure

- Chronic medical problems, such as asthma, may become uncontrolled.[30]

IDENTIFICATION THROUGH LAB TESTS

A drug abuser can be identified through lab testing. The drug or drugs being tested for varies depending on the testing company, how expensive the test is, what the person ordering the test plans to detect, and federal requirements. The person or company that wants the drug test done may require the testing be done for certain drugs. The Federal Government has guidelines created by the National Institute of Drug Abuse that mandate that all drug tests, at a minimum, screen for marijuana and cocaine. Federal guidelines also authorize testing for amphetamines, opiates, and phencyclidine, and so there are five main components to a drug test that all places of business should have. The five drugs screened for are

- Marijuana

- Cocaine

- Amphetamines (speed)

- Opiates (morphine or oxycodone)

- PCP (Angel Dust)[31,32]

Beyond this, testing can be done for many other drugs. Most companies do not test for all those listed below, but choose three or four of them instead:

- Barbiturates

- Hydrocodone (Vicodin)

- Quaaludes

- Benzodiazepines (Valium)

- Methadone

- Propoxyphene (Darvocet)

- Alcohol

- Ecstasy[33]

There are five different types of drug tests: urine, blood, hair, saliva, and sweat. Each one has different characteristics. By far the most common test is the urine test.

FAILING THE TEST

Brian had to have a drug test to get his first job. The company was really strict, and they required all new employees to have a hair-sample drug test. It didn't seem too bad; Brian just had to let someone cut some of his hair. He knew that he had taken some of those blue pills his friend Andy had, and he smoked pot, but he had stopped doing all that one month ago because he knew he would need to pass the test. But the hair sample easily showed his drug use over the past three months, and even being clean for one month didn't make a difference. Brian didn't get the job. And although he did get in trouble with his parents, he at least didn't get in trouble with the law.

Urine Drug Tests

- Are the least expensive

- Can be done at home by parents, but a lab must verify results

- Detect drug use within the past week

- Can be affected by not using drugs for a period before the test for a negative result

- Can be verified by temperature of the urine sample, which will be warm, versus a substitute sample from someone else, which will be cold

Saliva Tests

- Are more expensive than urine, but less expensive than blood

- Are becoming more popular

- Are very easy to give, but a lab must provide results

- Like urine tests, only detect drug use within a few days

- Are only starting to become more common, so the results are difficult to interpret, because there are no standard concentrations for detection, making the results less reliable than other methods

- Are most reliable for methamphetamines and opiates, but less reliable for marijuana than other tests

Hair Tests

- Are approximately seven times more expensive than urine tests

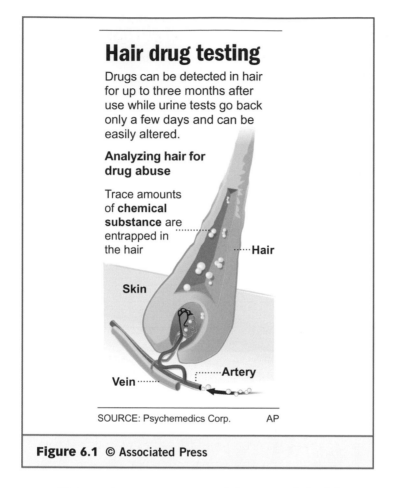

Hair drug testing

Drugs can be detected in hair for up to three months after use while urine tests go back only a few days and can be easily altered.

Analyzing hair for drug abuse

Trace amounts of **chemical substance** are entrapped in the hair

Hair

Skin

Vein

Artery

SOURCE: Psychemedics Corp.   AP

Figure 6.1 © Associated Press

- Detect substances over a much longer period of time (up to 90 days after use)

- Test positive for drugs twice as often as a urine test

- Can be used to determine when drug use occurred and if the drug has been discontinued

- Now test for the five main drug classes that are federally mandated and include at least marijuana, ecstasy, cocaine, opiates, methamphetamine, amphetamines, barbiturates, benzodiazepines, and PCP

Drugs, such as opiates (codeine, morphine, heroin) stick to the hair shaft and do not move along the length of the hair. If a long segment of hair is available one can draw some conclusions about when the drug use occurred. A drug such as cocaine, although very easy to detect, is able to move along the shaft. This makes it difficult to determine when the drug was used and for how long.

Blood Tests

- Are the most expensive

- The most accurate

- Least used due to expense

Sweat (Patch) Tests

- Are uncommon

- Are of unknown accuracy (Note: Some say that a patch test will probably not pick up an inhaled drug like marijuana.)

- Can detect drug use that would not trigger positive results with a urine test, such as single use of a variety of drugs within a week prior to using the patch

There are many situations in which a teen may be drug tested. This might first occur when one joins a school-sponsored sports team. In a number of school districts, teens must first pass a drug test to determine if they have used drugs in the past few days and, depending on the test, if they have used drugs within a month or two! When applying for a job, many companies require applicants to first take a physical, which includes a drug test. If the individual fails the drug test, he or she may not get the job! Companies do not want to hire someone who uses (or used) drugs and might come to work high or

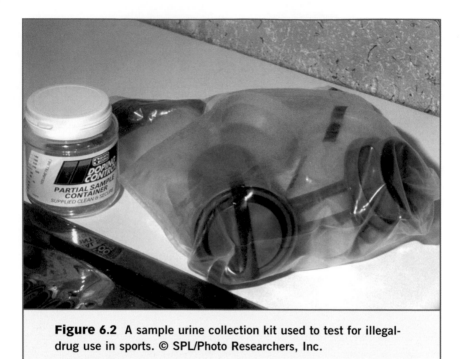

Figure 6.2 A sample urine collection kit used to test for illegal-drug use in sports. © SPL/Photo Researchers, Inc.

stoned. This can be harmful to their business and to their other employees.

Many Web sites claim to have products that will help people pass drug tests. They might offer certain natural or herbal medicines to get the drug out of the body faster or cover up drug use. These sites are untruthful. The detection of drugs is accurate. There really is no way to trick a test.

PREVENTION

People should strive to lead lives in which there is no reason to fear failing a drug test. There are a number of ways that you can help prevent drug abuse. One way is to get involved with Drug Abuse Resistance Education (D.A.R.E.). This year, 26 million kids in the United States will benefit from D.A.R.E., a program that gives kids the skills they need to avoid involvement in drugs, gangs, and violence.[34]

In many cases parents must begin the process of preventing drug abuse. But teens can participate in the education process, too, by involving their parents, and people with whom they are close, in their lives. Teens can talk to their parents about drug abuse. They can also talk to them if they think that a friend is abusing drugs. Parents were teenagers once themselves, and may know more about drug use than teens may think. They might even be able to share firsthand how drugs affected them when they were younger. Parents want to share their experiences so that teens can learn from them. Strong communication with parents is an important way to help teens stay away from drugs. So listen to your parents—they actually know a thing or two.

A parent of a friend can encourage schooling and stress how important it is not to abuse drugs. Communication should be open and honest. Even if your friend admits he or she is using drugs, don't think of this person as having a character flaw, and don't brand him or her as a "druggie." This is a friend who simply needs help, so help, don't hurt. A teen's friends or parents can encourage self-assertiveness through the simple statement "No." Everyone, be it a parent or teenager,

PRESSURE FOR POPULARITY

Jake was at a party where he didn't know many people, and while he was there, he was offered drugs. He didn't know what to do. The kids throwing the party were known as the *popular* kids. He didn't want to say no because he wanted to be accepted by them, and he might never have the chance to be part of that group if he turned them down. He was torn. He quickly made up the excuse, "I don't feel good, and taking that might make me feel worse." The popular kids didn't care at all, and Jake left the party quickly, relieved over his decision.

should remind themselves and those around them that using drugs is wrong and harmful. Everyone needs to have a personal commitment to not use drugs.[35]

It is also important to feel good about yourself. Think about a project that you worked on, a good grade that you received, or an important play you made at the last football or baseball game. Think about how you helped a family member in some way, even lifting heavy boxes for your mom. There are probably many people who are proud of you, even though you might not notice. And if you don't notice, then you should ask!

Always know for yourself, and encourage your friends, that it is okay to "Just say no." This may sound silly, but it is a simple and easy way to stop a friend from giving into peer pressure to try drugs. Make a pact or promise with your friends that each of you will avoid using drugs. Surround yourself with positive people. If you feel tempted or pressured by your friends, surround yourself with a new group of kids. Join a team sport. Many kids involved with sports or other school activities don't use drugs. They know that they can get caught through drug testing, and that their performance in the sport might be affected, which can make the whole team suffer.

Identification can come in two ways: by noticing signs of drug abuse in a friend and by the use of a drug test done by a lab. Identification might not come right away. A friend might be a user for a while before drug use is confirmed. This does not mean it is too late; simply noticing and starting to help a friend is the first step to their recovery. The simple act of prevention is equally if not more important. Having friends who stick together and help each other to stay clean means a lot to anyone who is pressured to use drugs.[36]

7

Treatment

TREATMENT OF DRUG ADDICTION

Most drug addicts do not realize that they have a problem. In the beginning, they think that they can easily stop abusing a drug. They might try many times to stop using their drug of choice, but fail to stay sober. Their brain thinks that they need the drug, therefore the abusers believes that they need the drug. Adequate treatment of drug abuse must come from many angles, and many different types of intervention must be used. Drug treatment must help a person stop using drugs and maintain a drug-free lifestyle that allows them to become a productive member of society, get along with their family, and keep and hold a job. Treatment must focus on the present drug abuse, but also help prevent a relapse, or future drug abuse.[37,38]

Drug addiction is a very complex disorder that can involve virtually every aspect of someone's life and affect every aspect of their daily living. Addiction is treated as a disease, and recovery from it benefits from a combination of psychotherapy, or counseling, and in certain cases, medication. The goal of counseling is to provide coping and training skills to help an abuser understand how to avoid drug use. Twelve-step programs such as Alcoholics Anonymous are weekly (or more frequent) behavioral interventions that address the underlying psychological reason for the patient's substance abuse problem. Medications target the chemical messengers, or biologic causes, responsible for the drug abuse, block the abusive substance's action, or reverse the chemical changes that cause the compulsion, craving, and loss of control characteristic of addiction. A combination of counseling and medication provides the best approach to the long-term treatment of drug abusers because it addresses both the social and biological problems responsible for the addiction.

There are many addictive drugs and specific treatments for different kinds of drug addictions are available. Treatment also varies according to the type of person who is an abuser. Many people have a drug abuse problem along with numerous other issues, such as mental health problems (like depression), health concerns, or other social problems. How bad their addiction is helps to define the type of drug treatment programs they require. Drug abuse treatment can involve three different modalities:

- **Psychotherapy**, also called counseling or behavior therapy

- **Drug therapy**

- Combination of both

EMERGENCY INTERVENTION

Jason was a drug abuser, according to his mom. He didn't see it. He liked to take pills every once in a while, but so what? He could stop whenever he wanted to, or so he thought. Soon Jason found that he needed the pills every week, then a few times a week, then every day, then multiple times each day. He still denied the fact that he was an abuser.

After one very long binge at a friend's apartment, he went home, passed out, and his mom found him. She took him to the hospital right away, and the doctors there said Jason needed help. He didn't want it, but since he was younger than 18, he had no choice. His mom made the decision for him to enter a drug rehabilitation program. After detoxification, which was an awful process, and a week of group therapy, he finally realized that he had a problem. It took two months in a special hospital for drug addicts before he was able to go home.

Drug abuse counselors determine which type of treatment is best for the patient.

BASICS OF THE TREATMENT OF DRUG ADDICTION

According to the National Institute of Drug Addiction (NIDA), there are basic principles for effective drug addiction treatment. There are two important things to remember:

- Treatment must involve different kinds of therapy (for example, mixed components of individual therapy, group therapy, and 12-step treatment programs).

- Drug abuse treatment lasts a lifetime.[39]

Treatment Principles:

- The type of therapy a patient needs is dependent on the person's individual problems and the type of drug that they used. Mental and psychological problems, and social and legal issues determine individual needs.

- Treatment must be available quickly. If treatment is not readily available and the person is ready to go into rehab, there is a good chance that the patient will be lost.

- The treatment plan must be assessed continually to make sure it meets the patient's changing needs.

- Treatment must be of an adequate duration of time.

- Counseling, both individual and group, is critical for effective treatment.

- Medications are important depending on the patient's addiction. (For barbiturates, there is no drug cure.)

- If medical detoxification is needed, it is only the first stage of treatment and does little to change long-term use.

- Recovery from drug addiction can be long-term and requires intervention throughout the years to help a person become fully drug free.

METHODS OF DRUG ABUSE REHABILITATION
Psychotherapy
Basic Principles of Psychotherapy

The underlying basis of all counseling for drug addiction is a focus on goals. These include short-term goals (such as getting clean), long-term goals (such as staying clean), behavioral goals, and goals directly related to addiction (such as knowing and understanding how to stay away from drugs). Patients also looks back on the past to help them realize what got them into drugs, and to the future to see that life will go on, that they can live a long, healthy, and very successful life no matter how bleak it looked like at one time.

Therapy for teenagers can differ slightly from that of adults. The basic principle of therapy is that the unwanted act of using drugs can be changed. This is done by showing what leading a clean life looks like, and depicting the rewards of being drug free. In therapy teens work through different activities and assignments, and rehearse those behaviors that go along with being drug free. A teen's progress must be tracked and reviewed regularly, with praise and privileges given for meeting his or her goals. Urine samples are collected regularly, without advance notice. There are three goals associated with therapy for teens:

1. *Stimulus control:* This helps the patient avoid environments associated with drug use, such as going to raves. It stresses the importance of staying away from peer-pressure situations.

2. *Urge control:* This helps patients realize and change the thoughts, feelings, and plans that lead to drug use.

3. *Social control:* This involves the teen's family and other people who are important to them. A parent attends all treatment sessions with the teen to help keep the person on track with their drug-free life. The more praise that drug abusers get, the more they believe they can keep off drugs.

Research shows that this kind of therapy really helps teens to become drug free and increases their ability to remain so after their therapy ends. It also shows that they demonstrate improvement in other areas of their life. They go to school all of the time, are able to be more productive at their jobs, enjoy a much better home life, and have a decrease in depression that they might otherwise feel.

There are multiple ways in which the family and friends are involved in an outpatient drug rehabilitation program. Treatment includes individual and family counseling sessions held at a clinic, school, in family court, or another location in their community (e.g., a church or town hall). During these sessions parents learn how they can help with the process of staying clean. Their parenting skills are examined by counselors to make sure that they are not one of the sources of the problem and that they understand what's involved in reestablishing mutual trust with their child.[40]

During individual sessions the therapist and teenager work on developing decision-making and problem-solving skills. Teens who develop strong communication skills and are better able to cope with difficult choices and challenges have a higher likelihood of becoming and staying drug free. This type of treatment can be intense at times, but it is very effective and raises the probability that the teen will stop using and get away from drugs. Consequently there is also less of a chance that the teen will commit crimes or engage in other negative activities.

Overall, behavior therapy can help with many of the negative things that can happen when a teen uses drugs. It can renew one's ability to have a positive family life, in which there is open communication and an understanding by all that there was a problem and there may always be, but that the family will get through it together. Friendships can be restored following therapy, and the days of lying to friends can be ended. For both friends and family, there can be a renewed sense of security that there will no more stealing from them.

GENERAL CATEGORIES OF INPATIENT DRUG TREATMENT PROGRAMS

There are three main types of drug treatment programs available. They are: **outpatient drug-free treatment**, **long-term residential programs**, and **short-term residential programs**. The activities that an inpatient drug program incorporates are usually medical detoxification plus individual and group counseling.

COUNSELING HELPS

Brian was 16 years old and found himself in a huge rut. His school had screened him for drugs when he tried to join the football team, and when the results came back positive, the school mandated that he and his parents go to counseling. He didn't like it. The sessions made Brian realize all of the things about himself that he didn't like. They showed him that he had poor self-esteem and little respect for his body. He hated therapy, and as much as he hated it, so did his parents. It was difficult for them to hear how they were not there for their son, and how they didn't realize the signs of drug abuse. After a few sessions, though, they understood how they could help him, both now and in the future. Although counseling was not easy, Brian and his parents learned from their mistakes, and more importantly, they learned how to make things better for the future.

Figure 7.1 Components of comprehensive drug abuse treatment.

Long Term Rehabilitation

This type of therapy gives care 24 hours a day, usually in a rehab facility, not a hospital. The length of stay at each program and for each person varies; most are approximately 6 to 12 months. Long-term rehab can be thought of as a *community* of drug addicts. During treatment, a patient is exposed to other people who have an addiction so that they can gain an understanding of why they became addicted, and learn how they are coping with addiction treatment. This is completed by one-on-one counseling and group counseling sessions.

Short Term Rehab

These programs are intense, but of a shorter duration than a long-term program. They encompass most of the basic principles involved with long-term therapy. Short-term programs are no less effective than long-term programs, but many no longer exist, mainly due lack of financing, in part having to do with the difficulty in getting adequate reimbursement from insurance companies.

Outpatient Drug Rehabilitation

Outpatient drug rehabilitation is useful for patients who have jobs, are in school, and who have a very good support system, especially at home. Their addiction must not be classified as serious and they cannot require medical detoxification from their drug of abuse. Many outpatient programs emphasize group therapy. Some programs are designed to treat not only someone's drug addiction but a mental disorder as well. Outpatient rehab programs can be just as effective as inpatient programs, depending on the patient and his or her motivation and support system.

DRUG TREATMENT OF ABUSE

There are no drugs that can be used in the treatment of barbiturate abuse or addiction, but it is good to have some knowledge of those available to treat other addictions. For a friend or parent addicted to another drug, there may be legal drugs they can take to help them kick the habit.

Drugs like Narcan® (naloxone) are used when someone overdoses on morphine. Methadone is a narcotic medication that helps heroin or opioid abusers stop using their drug of choice by replacing it with a legal and well-controlled one. ReVia® (naltrexone) is used as a deterrent to opioid use, and there are other drugs available for this, such as Subutex® (buprenorphine) and Subuxone® (buprenorphine and naloxone). A drug called Antabuse® (disulfiram) can be used to deter an alcoholic from taking alcohol.[41]

ReVia blocks the effects of opioids by competing with these drugs for opioid receptors in the brain. It was originally used to treat dependence on opioid drugs but has recently been approved by the FDA as treatment for alcoholism. Patients who receive ReVia are twice as successful in remaining drug free and in avoiding relapse.

Methadone is used for the treatment of narcotic withdrawal and dependence. It occupies the opioid receptor in the brain and is the stabilizing factor that permits addicts to change their behavior and to discontinue heroin use. Methadone suppresses narcotic withdrawal for between 24 and 36 hours, and because it is effective in eliminating withdrawal symptoms, it is used in detoxifying opiate addicts. Ultimately, the patient remains physically dependent on the opioid, but is freed from the uncontrolled, compulsive, and disruptive behavior seen in heroin addicts.[42]

Antabuse helps people who have an addiction to alcohol, not by working against alcohol, but by causing a bad reaction when someone who is taking the medication drinks anything alcoholic. Someone on Antabuse who drinks alcohol will experience

- Vomiting
- Flushing of the skin
- Throbbing head and neck
- Throbbing headache
- Sweating
- Chest pain
- Pounding heart beat
- Fast heart rate
- Low blood pressure
- Weakness
- Dizziness

Figure 7.2 A counselor talks to adolescents at a chemical dependency support group. © Lawrence Migdale/Photo Researchers, Inc.

Subutex (buprenorphine) and Suboxone (buprenorphine/naloxone) are legal medications used to treat addiction to opioids. Buprenorphine prevents withdrawal symptoms. Subutex contains only the medicine buprenorphine, while Suboxone contains naloxone as well. When naloxone is injected or taken as a pill, it blocks the effects of medicines and drugs, such as heroin and morphine. Naloxone is added to Suboxone to stop people from injecting, or shooting-up.

Other types of medications may be used to treat people going through drug abuse treatment for anxiety that may develop or for any sort of psychological problems the patient may have. So while no drugs are available to directly treat barbiturate addiction, a patient suffering from barbiturate abuse and depression or bipolar disorder might be helped by medications to treat their mental health problems.

CONCLUSION

There are many ways to treat someone for drug addiction. The first step is on the part of the abusers. They must recognize they have a problem. A few of the primary principles of drug treatment are: No single treatment is appropriate for all patients. The treatment plan must be continually assessed to ensure the patient's needs are met. Counseling (individual or group) is critical to the effective treatment of addiction. Rehab is not an easy process. Recovering drug abusers face not only the physical effects but also the mental aspects of ending addiction. Many patients find it difficult to go through counseling, but therapy is essential because the patient must learn about themselves, their addiction, and how they must act in the future. It is not an easy thing to do, but it is important for all of those people involved in a patient's life to support them in every way possible.

8

The Future

Drug abuse is not an easy topic to discuss. The negative effects it can have on your body are unpleasant to think about. Treating a drug addiction might temporarily make someone feel even worse. The overall idea to understand is that it is just as important, if not more so, to prevent drug abuse, and avoid the unhealthy consequences. Prevention is better from a legal standpoint, too, because drugs can get you into big trouble. The United States government has different laws that prohibit acquiring, using, or distributing drugs.

BACKGROUND ON JUSTICE

In the United States the Drug Enforcement Administration (DEA) is the main governing body for the Controlled Substances Act, a federal law. The DEA, part of the Department of Justice, monitors the legal drug trade for people like pharmacists and physicians. It also heads the agency that coordinates the effort to stop domestic and international illegal drug trafficking.[43]

The Controlled Substances Act is set up to limit and control access to drugs that can make you high, and other drugs of abuse, such as anabolic steroids used by athletes to increase muscle mass. The DEA decides which drugs are controlled substances. Conversely, the Food and Drug Administration decides which drugs are available by prescription. The Controlled Substances Act allows for tight control of drugs of abuse by placing all controlled drugs into five classes and requiring health care professionals such as doctors and pharmacists to register with the DEA.[44]

At the time the Controlled Substances Act was passed in 1970, abuse of drugs was out of control. It was estimated that nearly 50 percent of all legally produced amphetamines and barbiturates were being diverted into the black market. Legally produced drugs were a major part of the drug abuse problem in the United States, by some estimates making up as much as 90 percent of the illicit drugs on the street. There was no one single cause for the problem, but the nature of illicit drug trafficking depends largely on the availability of drugs or the

DRUGS, GAMBLING, JAIL

Greg was addicted to drugs, and to buy those little blue pills that he loved, he needed a lot of money, fast. Greg loved sports, and he knew how he could make money by betting on them. He started slowly, by making bets with his friends at school for 10 dollars, but he didn't make enough money to support his habit. His friend Pete introduced him to his Dad's football bookie, and soon, Greg started to bet hundreds of dollars at a time. He was living the high life while his luck held, and he had more than enough money to keep up his drug habit.

Before long, though, he got a little too sure of himself, and made a really big bet. He lost all of his money, and then owed the bookie more than a thousand dollars. He had nowhere to turn and couldn't tell anyone, especially his parents, that he was in gambling trouble, ultimately because of his addiction. Getting a job at the local grocery store wasn't going to cut it. So his friend Pete's brother offered to help him out if Greg agreed to sell some pills. This way he could make money, and make it fast to pay off his debts. Greg made a few deals, but got caught. He went to jail on drug charges, had to pay a huge fine, complete community service, and wound up with a permanent mark on his record.

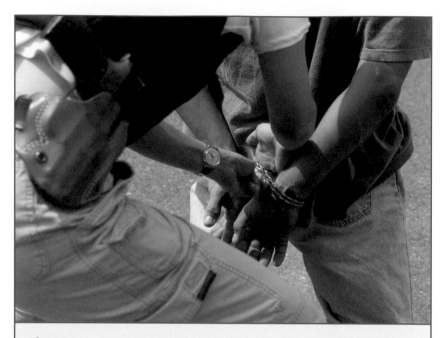

Figure 8.1 Law enforcement agents enforce laws regarding controlled substances and arrest drug dealers, suppliers, and users. © Anna Clopet/Corbis

chemicals required for making them from legal sources. Many recent laws and programs have been extended to the chemicals required for secretly manufacturing drugs of abuse.

DIVERSION OF CONTROLLED PHARMACEUTICALS

Many of the narcotics, depressants, and stimulants made for proper, legal medical use are subject to abuse, and have therefore been brought under legal control. The goal of control is to ensure that these substances are readily available for medical use, while preventing their distribution for illegal sale and abuse. Under federal law, all businesses that manufacture or distribute controlled drugs; all health professionals allowed to dispense, administer, or prescribe them; and all pharmacies entitled to fill prescriptions must register with the DEA. Registrants must obey a series of regulations relating to drug security, drug records accountability, and adherence to all standards that are part of federal law.

Diversion cases involve, but are not limited to: physicians who sell prescriptions to drug dealers or abusers, pharmacists who falsify records and subsequently sell drugs, employees who steal from inventory at a pharmacy, executives of drug companies who falsify orders to cover illicit sales, and the use of fake prescriptions. At present, the largest problem results from the criminal activity of physicians and pharmacy personnel.

DRUG SCHEDULING / CLASSES OF DRUGS

The DEA has determined the scheduling of drugs. The drug is assigned a category from I to V. The higher the addiction potential and the less safe the drug, the lower the schedule. (Heroin, for instance, is a Schedule I drug.)

1. Schedule I drugs have a high potential for abuse, with no accepted medical use. Schedule I drugs include, but are not limited to, heroin, marijuana, and other hallucinogens.

2. Schedule II drugs have a high potential for abuse, but some medical use, and include, morphine, codeine, barbiturates, and amphetamines.

3. Schedule III, Schedule IV and Schedule V drugs have some potential for abuse, but less than Schedule I and II drugs, with Schedule III drugs having the most potential for abuse and Schedule V the least. Schedule III, IV and V drugs include certain barbiturates (III and IV), and benzodiazines (Valium or Xanax) (III and IV).[45]

LAW

Most states have passed their own laws that are much like the Controlled Substances Act, although there are differences from state to state. As a rule a state can add restrictions to the federal law, but can never reduce a sentence based on it due to required mandatory minimums. The nature of drug charges varies by state. In some states a 14 year old can be charged as an adult for a drug crime. In others, those who distribute drugs to someone under the age of 18 can get twice the usual fine or jail time for distributing to someone older than 18. The term *distribute* does not mean just selling a drug. Simply passing off a drug to someone can be considered distribution, even when no money passes through hands.

Drug possession is usually a felony. Illegal drug possession comes with steeper penalties when the drug has a higher potential for addiction, physical harm, and death. Illegal drug possession is also a more serious crime when a person has a greater quantity of an illegal substance. Offenders who are caught with large amounts of illegal drugs may be charged with possession with the intent to distribute, a crime that carries harsher legal implications.

Illegal drug possession penalties are also greater for those individuals who have had a prior illegal drug possession conviction. These offenders often face a harsher penalty, which may include an increased period of jail time and higher fines. Penalties are also steeper in cases where the offender was in close proximity to a day care center, school, or university at the time of arrest. Drug possession can result in a sentence that includes jail or prison time, fines, probation, attending drug treatment programs, and other penalties.[46]

Federal laws set the following fines and penalties for trafficking drugs:

- *Schedule I and II Drugs:* For the first offense, the penalty is from 5 to 40 years imprisonment and/or not more than a $2 million fine for an individual. In cases when death or serious injury occurs, the sentence may be not less than 20 years imprisonment and not more than life imprisonment. For a second drug offense, federal law states that someone should not spend less than 10 years imprisonment and not more than life and/or a fine of not less than $4 million for an individual. In cases where death or serious injury occurs, they should be sentenced to life in prison.

- *Schedule III Drug:* Jail time is not longer that five years, with or without a $250,000 fine for a first offense; penalty is doubled for a second offense.

- *Schedule IV Drug:* Jail time is not longer than three years, with or without a $250,000 fine for a first offense; penalty is doubled for a second offense.

- *Schedule V Drug:* Jail time is not longer than one year, with or without a $100,000 fine for a first offense; penalty is doubled for a second offense.[47]

As you can see, the penalties for drug use, carrying a drug, or selling drugs are steep. If you are charged with a drug-related offense, when you apply for student loans or grants in the future you might be denied, and you might not be eligible for some jobs.

FIRST OFFENSE

Jennifer was a good student and a member of the school marching band and drama club. Her friend Dave asked her to hold onto a bag that he had. The bag was sealed, so she didn't know what was in it. As she was walking down the hallway in school, the bag fell and split open, spilling out a bunch of pills that turned out to be barbiturates. Jennifer didn't know what they were or why Dave had them, but it didn't matter to her school, the police, or the judge in court. Jennifer was not sentenced to jail, but she had to pay a $10,000 fine for possession of illegal drugs.

Figure 8.2 Many schools have instituted actions and programs intended to eradicate drugs from the school ground and community. © Joseph Sohm; ChromoSohm Inc./Corbis

MEDICATIONS IN DEVELOPMENT

Medication development for use in drug addiction has focused on the need to detoxify, treat withdrawal symptoms, make possible a smooth recovery, and prevent future drug use. Currently available medications include substitutes where a "street" drug is replaced with a "clean" drug (such as methadone); blockers that prevent the addictive substance from having any "good feeling" effects (such as naltrexone); or aversive therapies (such as disulfiram, which makes you feel sick if you take it with alcohol.) Because it can be extremely difficult for addicted patients to continue to take their medications every day, there is a need for drugs with less frequent dosing schedules to increase the likelihood the patient stays on them. There is also an important

need for effective treatments for cocaine and methamphetamine overdoses, as none are currently available. A long-term
goal is to develop medications that help keep abusive substances out of the brain to help prevent their addictive effects
and consequences.[48]

OUTLOOK AND CONCLUSION

With aggressive treatment in the hospital and counseling, most
people survive barbiturate abuse. However, even with aggressive therapy, some patients die. A person's outcome after abusing barbiturates depends on many factors, such as:

- The other drugs that are taken with the barbiturate

- Other medical problems the patient may have

- How quickly he or she seeks and receives medical
  attention

- The type of barbiturate he or she has abused

The judicial consequences are also quite severe. Preventing
drug abuse is important, but if someone does get mixed up
with drug abuse, identifying and supporting them are the first
steps to recovery. Detoxification and rehabilitation follow.
Finally, preventing future drug use and keeping clean is the
ultimate goal of therapy. Once a person is a drug addict, that
tendency can stay with him or her for the rest of his or her life.
Addictive behavior can be recognized and curbed, however,
through ongoing support and knowledge.

Glossary

activated charcoal—Thick, black carbon derived mainly from charcoal and used block absorption of drugs in the digestive tract.

Adderall—Trade name for amphetamine-dextramphetamine, a potentially habit-forming stimulant used to treat ATTENTION-DEFICIT/HYPERACTIVITY DISORDERS

alprazolam—A BENZODIAZIPENE drug used to treat anxiety disorders and panic attacks.

amobarbital—A BARBITURATE used for diagnostic purposes prior to brain surgery.

analgesia—Pain-relieving; analgesic drugs are used to manage pain.

anticonvulsant—Capable of preventing or controlling convulsions or seizures.

attention-deficit/hyperactivity disorder (ADHD)—A condition marked by nervousness, hyperactivity, inattention, and inappropriate, impulsive behavior. ADHD can interfere with learning and social development. Most commonly diagnosed during childhood and treated with drugs such as RITALIN.

Barbital—Trade name for 5.5-diethylbarbituric acid, a HYPNOTIC/SEDATIVE drug produced by Emil Fischer.

barbiturates—Central nervous system depressants discovered in 1863, and now mainly used for anesthesia or to treat epilepsy.

barbituric acid—An organic compound that provides the basis for BARBITURATES.

benzodiazepines—Drugs with anticonvulsive, hypnotic, and sedative properties, used to treat insomnia or for anesthetic purposes. There are three classes: short-acting, intermediate-acting, and long-acting.

central nervous system depressants—Drugs that diminish or slow down brain activity, affecting mainly voluntary actions, but also involuntary ones at higher doses.

corticosteriods—A class of steroid hormones produced in the body; synthetic corticosteriods are used for a variety of medical purposes. Their effectiveness diminishes when combined with BARBITURATES.

chronic use—Use of a drug on a regular basis.

delirium tremens—Anxiety, insomnia, tremors, and other adverse affects associated with alcohol withdrawal.

disorientation—Lack of awareness of one's surroundings, situation, or even basic information such as the time or one's name.

Dorminal—Trade name for 5.5-diethylbarbituric acid, a HYPNOTIC/SEDATIVE drug produced by Emil Fischer.

doxycycline—An antibiotic used to treat gum disease. Its effectiveness diminishes when combined with BARBITURATES.

drug therapy—Use of drugs to aid in addiction recovery, alter a patient's behavior, and improve a patient's emotional and mental state.

epilepsy—A neurological condition that causes chronic periods of unprovoked convulsions or seizures. It can be treated with drugs or surgery.

euphoria—An extreme sensation of joy and well-being, sometimes sought through drug abuse.

exaggerated personality—A sudden change in personality, such as when a normally quiet or calm person becomes hyperactive, impulsive, loud, or obnoxious, usually under the influence of alcohol or drugs.

febrile seizures—Seizures associated with very high fevers; most common in infants.

GABA receptors—Brain and nervous system messengers that control body functions by slowing them when activated.

gateway drugs—Relatively mild drugs that abusers use before turning to harder or more powerful drugs in order to get high. Gateway drugs are often legal or easy to come by, such as alcohol, marijuana, or tobacco.

hypnotic—A class of sleep-inducing drugs used to treat insomnia.

Impotence—Inability of a man to achieve erection due to physiological or psychological factors.

insomnia—Difficulty achieving or inability to sleep.

intermediate-acting—Drug effects that last for approximately 6 to 8 hours.

in utero—Within a woman's uterus.

long-acting—Drug effects that last for an extended period of time, such as 10 to 16 hours.

long-term residential programs—A drug recovery program in which a patient receives round the clock care while staying in a hospital or rehabilitation facility for 6 to 12 months.

malonic acid—An acid found in fruit and combined with UREA to create BARBITURIC ACID.

methohexital—A BARBITURATE used for diagnostic purposes prior to brain surgery.

naloxone—A drug used to treat overdoses of narcotics like morphine.

narcolepsy—A neurological condition that causes extreme sleepiness at inappropriate times.

narrow therapeutic index drugs—Drugs with a very small line between what amount constitutes a therapeutic dose and a potentially lethal overdose.

Glossary

opioids—A chemical that binds to opioid receptors in the central nervous system. The human body naturally manufacturers certain opioids; synthetic opioids include drugs such as codeine, heroin, and morphine.

outpatient drug-free treatment—A drug recovery program in which a patient receives care while living at home and continuing to work and take part in his or her life.

Oxycontin—Trade name for the pain-relief drug oxycodone and hydrochloride, which can be addictive.

phenobarbital—A BARBITUATE used to control anxiety and epilepsy. Popular in the past, it has largely been supplanted by newer drugs, though it is still commonly used to treat animals.

potassium bromide—An old seizure medication, sometimes used in combination with phenobarbital, now mainly used to treat animals.

psychotherapy—Counseling intended to aid in drug rehabilitation, alter a patient's behavior, and improve a patient's emotional and mental state.

psychoactive substances—A chemical that alters mental processes to affect behavior, mood, or perception.

Ritalin—Trade name for the stimulant methylphenidate, used to treat attention-deficit/hyperactivity disorder. It is abused because its pharmacological effects are similar to those of other stimulants like amphetamines and cocaine.

sedative—A drug that causes relaxation and suppresses anxiety by depressing the central nervous system.

seizure focus—The location in an epileptic patient's brain that is responsible for causing seizures.

short-acting—Drug affects that last from 3 to 4 hours.

short-term residential programs—An intensive drug recovery program in which a patient receives care while at a hospital or rehabilitation facility for several weeks.

Status Epilepticus—A life-endangering form of seizure, during which an epileptic's seizure may last for several minutes or hours rather than several seconds.

stimulants—Drugs that increase or speed up activity of the nervous system.

street drugs—Unregulated, illegal drugs commonly available for sale on the street. Such drugs are not subject to quality standards and may vary widely in potency and content.

Veronal—Trade name for 5.5-diethylbarbituric acid, a HYPNOTIC/SEDATIVE drug produced by Emil Fischer.

Vicodin—A pain-relief drug that combines acetaminophen with hydrocodone, which can be habit-forming.

urea—A compound of carbon, hydrogen, nitrogen, and oxygen found in urine.

Xanax—A brand name for ALPRAZOLAM.

Further Reading

Clayton, Lawrence. *Barbiturates and Other Depressants.* (Drug Abuse Prevention Library). New York: Rosen Publishing Group, 2001.

Houle, Michelle M. *Tranquilizer, Barbiturate, and Downer Drug Dangers.* (Drug Dangers). Berkeley Heights, N.J.: Enslow Publishers, 2001.

Koda-Kimble, MA et al. (eds.). *Applied Therapeutics: The Clinical Use of Drugs.* Baltimore: Lippincott, Williams and Wilkins, 2005

National Institutes of Health, National Institute on Drug Abuse. http://www.nida.nih.gov/.

U.S. Department of Health and Human Services, and SAMHSA's National Clearinghouse for Alcohol & Drug Information. http://www.health.org.

U.S. Department of Justice, Drug Enforcement Administration, Office of Diversion Control. http://www.deadiversion.usdoj.gov.

Web Sites

American Academy of Pediatrics
http://www.aap.org

Drug Enforcement Agency
http://www.dea.gov

Partnership for a Drug-Free America
http://www.drugfree.org

Shands Healthcare Information
http://www.shands.org/health/information

Endnotes

1 *Pharmacy Today.* "Medication abuse a growing problem among the nations youth." Pharmacy Today on the Web. Available online. URL: http://www.pharmacist.com/pdf/PT/200506_drugcover.pdf. Accessed May 25, 2006.

2 National Institute on Drug Abuse. http://www.nida.nih.gov/infofacts/HSYouthtrends.html. Accessed on March 18, 2006.

3 The National Library of Medicine. "DSM-IV Criteria for Substance-Related Disorders." Available online. URL: http://www.ncbi.nlm.nih.gov/ entrez/query.fcgi?cmd=Search&db=books&doptcmdl=GenBookHL&term= DSM-IV+Criteria+for+Substance- Related+Disorders+AND+324523%5Buid%5D&rid=hstat5.section. 45624#45674 Downloaded on May 25, 2006.

4 National Institute on Drug Abuse. "Diagnosis and treatment of drug abuse in family practice." Available online. URL: http://www.drugabuse.gov/ Diagnosis-Treatment/Diagnosis.html. Accessed on May 25, 2006.

5 U.S. Drug Enforcement Administration. "Controlled Substances Act." Available online. URL: http://www.usdoj.gov/dea/agency/csa.htm. Accessed March 18, 2006.

6 U.S. Department of Health and Human Services and SAMHSA's National Clearinghouse for Alcohol and Drug Information. http://www.health.org.

7 Cherubin, C. E., and J. D. Sapira. "The medical complications of drug addiction and the medical assessment of the intravenous drug user: Twenty five years later. *Animals of Internal Medicine* 119 (1993):1017–1028.

8 Thomson Micromedex. http://www.thomsonhc.com. Accessed December 20, 2006.

9 Hardman, J. G., et al. eds. *Goodman & Gilman's: The Pharmacological Basis of Therapeutics.* 9th ed. New York: McGraw-Hill, 1996.

10 IK, Ho, and R. A. Harris. "Mechanism of action of barbiturates." *Annual Review of Pharmacology and Toxicology* 23 (1981): 83–111.

11 American Hospital Formulary Service. "Current drug therapy— barbiturates." *American Journal of Hospital Pharmacy* 33 (1976): 333–339.

12 Lopez-Munoz, F., R. Ucha-Udabe, and C. Alamo. "The history of barbiturates a century after their clinical introduction." *Neuropsych Disease and Treatment* 1, no. 4 (2005): 329–343.

13 Smith, M. C., and B. J. Risking. "The clinical use of barbiturates in neurological disorders." *Drugs* 42, no. 3 (1991): 365–378.

14 Spear, P. W. and L. M. Protass. "Barbiturate poisoning—an endemic disease." The Medical Clinics of North America, 57 (1973): 1471–1479.

15 DiPiro, J. T., et al. eds. *Pharmacotherapy: A Pathophysiologic Approach.* New York: McGraw-Hill Medical Publishing, 2005.

16 Kastrup, E. K., *Drug Facts and Comparisons.* St Louis: Wolters Kluwers Health, 2005.

17 Kastrup, E. K., ed. "Sedatives and Hypnotics, Barbiturates." *Drug Facts and Comparisons*. St. Louis: Wolters Kluwers Health, 2005. 977–984.

18 Schachter, S. C. "Overview of the management of epilepsy in adults." URL: http://www.uptodate.com (available by subscription only). Accessed July 28, 2005.

19 Veterinary Medicine Web site. Available online. URL: http://vetmedicine.about.com. Accessed March 18, 2006.

20 Parker, Jim. "Barbiturates: Show Stoppers." Available online. URL: http://www.doitnow.org/pages/111.html. Downloaded on February 24, 2005.

21 Romero, C. E. et al. "Barbiturate Withdrawal Following Internet Purchase of Fioricet." *Archives of Neurology* 61 (2004): 1111–1112.

22 Hardman, J. G., L. E. Limbard, and A. G. Gilman. *Goodman & Gilman's: The Pharmacological Basis of Therapeutics.* 10th ed. New York: McGraw-Hill, 2001.

23 Helpguide.org. "Drug Abuse and Addiction: Signs, Symptoms, Effects and Testing." Available online. URL: http://www.helpguide.org/mental/drug_substance_abuse_addiction_signs_effects_treatment.htm. Downloaded on February 24, 2006.

24 Doering, P. L. "Substance-Related Disorders: Overview and Depressants, Simulants and Hallucinogen." *Pharmacotherapy: A Pathophysiologic Approach.* 4th ed. Stamford, Conn.: Appleton and Lange, 1999.

25 Khantzian, E. J., and G. J. McKenna. "Acute toxic and withdrawal reactions associated with drug use and abuse." Annals of Internal Medicine 90 (1979): 361–372.

26 Teen Drug Abuse. "Teen drug abuse and the effects on the family." Available online. URL: http://www.teendrugabuse.us/DrugsNFamily.html accessed. Accessed May 25, 2006.

27 Free Vibe. "Step Up." Available online. URL: http://www.freevibe.com/stepup/pdfs/stepupbrochure.pdf. Downloaded February 25, 2006.

28 DEA Demand Reduction, Street Smart Prevention. "Costs to Society." Available online. URL: http://www.justthinktwice.com/costs/. Downloaded February 27, 2006.

29 Galloway, J. H., and I. D. Marsh. "Detection of drug misuse—an addictive challenge." *Journal of Clinical Pathology* 52 (1999): 713–718.

30 Mersy, D. J. "Recognition of Alcohol and Substance Abuse." *American Family Physician* 67 (2003): 1529–1532.

31 United States Department of Health and Human Services, Substance Abuse and Mental Health Service Administration, Division of Workplace Programs. "Drug Testing—Urine Drug Testing." Available online. URL: http://workplace.samhsa.gov/DrugTesting/Background.htm. Downloaded February 27, 2006.

Endnotes

32 United States Department of Health and Human Services, Substance Abuse and Mental Health Service Administration, Division of Workplace Programs. "Drug Cutoff Concentrations." Available online. URL: http://dwp.samhsa.gov/DrugTesting/Files_Drug_Testing/Labs/Drug%20Cut off%20Concentrations%20-%20February%202005.pdf. Downloaded February 27, 2006.

33 The Vaults of Erowid. "Drug Testing Basics." Available online. URL: http://www.erowid.org/psychoactives/testing/testing_info1.shtml. Downloaded February 27, 2006.

34 Drug Abuse Resistance Education (D.A.R.E.). "About D.A.R.E." Available online. URL: http://www.dare.com/home/about_dare.asp. Downloaded February 27, 2006.

35 National Institutes of Health, National Institute on Drug Abuse, U.S. Department of Health and Human Services. "Preventing Drug Abuse among Children and Adolescents." Available online. URL: http://www. drugabuse.gov/pdf/prevention/InBrief.pdf. Downloaded February 27, 2006.

36 Warning Signs. "Drug and Alcohol Prevention Tips." Available online. URL: http://www.warningsigns.info/drugs_prevention_tips_PDFA.htm. Accessed May 25, 2006.

37 Carroll, K. M. "Integrating psychotherapy and pharmacotherapy to improve drug abuse outcomes." *Addictive Behavior* 22 (1997): 233–245.

38 Barry, J. Dave and Christopher Beach. "Barbiturate Abuse." Available online. URL: http://www.emedicinehealth.com/barbiturate_abuse/article_em.htm. Downloaded February 28, 2006.

39 National Institutes of Health, National Institute on Drug Abuse, U.S. Department of Health and Human Services. "Principles of Drug Addiction Treatment: A Research-Based Guide." Available online. URL: http://www.drugabuse.gov/PDF/PODAT/PODAT.pdf. Downloaded February 28, 2006.

40 Pratter, C. D., K. E. Miller, and R. G. Zylstra . "Outpatient detoxification of the addicted alcoholic patient." *American Family Physican.* 60 (1999): 1200–1205.

41 Disulfiram (Antabuse). Lexi-Comp Drug Information Database. Lexi-Comp, Inc. Online Drug Information Database (available by subscription only). Monograph updated January 30, 2006.

42 Skinner, M. H., and D. A. Thompson. "Pharmacologic considerations in the treatment of substance abuse." *Southern Medical Journal* 85 (1992): 1217–1219.

43 U.S. Department of Justice, Drug Enforcement Administration, Office of Diversion Control. "The Diversion of Drugs and Chemicals." Available online. URL: http://www.deadiversion.usdoj.gov/pubs/program/activities/introduction. htm. Downloaded February 28, 2006.

44 U.S. Department of Justice, Drug Enforcement Administration, Office of Diversion Control. "Program Description." Available online. URL: http://www.deadiversion.usdoj.gov/prog_dscrpt/index.html. Downloaded February 28. 2006.

45 Federal Law. (21 USC §844)S

46 Online Lawyer Source. "Illegal Drug Possession." Available online. URL: http://www.onlinelawyersource.com/criminal_law/drug-possession/illegal.html. Downloaded March 2, 2006.

47 U.S. Drug Enforcement Administration. "Federal Trafficking Penalties." Available online. URL: http://www.dea.gov/agency/penalties.htm. Downloaded February 28, 2006.

48 PhRMA: New Medicines, New Hope. New Medicines Database. "Drug Abuse." Available online. URL: http://newmeds.phrma.org/results.php? indication=262. Downloaded February 28, 2006.

Index

Index

hair tests, 60, 61–63
hallucination, 54
hallucinogens, 81
hangover, 22
Harrison Narcotic Act, 7
Hauptmann, Alfred,
32–33
heart, infection of, 48
heroin, 35, 63, 75, 81
high. *See* euphoria
HIV. *See* human immun-
odeficiency virus
Hobbes, Thomas, 6
human immunodeficien-
cy virus (HIV), 18, 48,
57
hydrocodone, 15, 60
hydromorphone, 15
hygiene, poor, 48, 49
hypnotic, 32, 41

identification and prevention of abuse
identification of drug
abuser, 57–59
lab tests, 59–64
prevention, 64–66
reasons for, 55–57
illegal use of barbiturates
acquiring drugs,
44–47
reasons for abuse, 44
symptoms of abuse,
47—48
tolerance, 48
toxic and overdose reac-
tions, 49–50
treatment of overdose,
50–51
withdrawal, 51–54
illicit drugs, 10, 16
impotence, 34
infection, 48
inhalants, 11
injuries, accidental, 49, 59
inpatient drug treatment
programs, 72–73

long-term residential,
73
outpatient drug rehabil-
itation, 74
short-term residential,
73–74
insomnia, 41, 43. *See also*
sleep disorders
interactions, drug-drug,
27–27
intermediate-acting bar-
biturate, 39, 40
intravenous (IV) form, 48
in utero exposure to barbiturates, 29
irritability, 52
IV form. *See* intravenous
form

judgement, impaired, 34,
50

lab tests, identification of
drug abuse, 59–60, 66
blood tests, 63
hair tests, 61–63
saliva tests, 61
sweat (patch) tests,
63–64
urine drug tests,
61, 64
legal issues, 81–84
liver, enlarged, 59
long-acting barbiturate,
39, 40, 41
long-term residential, 73
lorazepam, 15
Luminal, 32, 40
lying, 47, 49, 55, 72

magnetic resonance
image (MRI), 43
malonic acid, 30
marijuana
ancient uses of, 6
gateway drug, 16
illegal drug, 45

investigational
purposes, use for, 35
Schedule I drug, 81
testing for, 59, 61, 62
trends in use, 11
Mebaral, 40
medical uses of barbitu-
rates, 30
alcohol withdrawal, 43
chemical structure,
30–32
classification of barbiturates, 39–41
current medical uses of,
38
diagnostic testing,
42–43
history, 32–37
sedative/hypnotics, 41
seizures, 41–42
veterinary uses, 42
medications in develop-
ment, 84–85
memory, impaired, 34, 54
mental disorders, 12
meperidine, 15
mephobarbital, 40, 41
Mering, Joseph von, 32
methadone, 15, 60, 75, 84
methamphetamines, 12,
61, 62, 85
methohexital, 40, 42
methylphenidate, 15
migraine headaches, 24,
47
misuse of prescription
drugs. *See* prescription
drug abuse and mis-
use
mood swings, 47, 53, 58
morphine
commonly abused pre-
scription drug, 15
overdose, 50, 74
Schedule II drug, 81
testing for, 59, 63
motivation, lack of, 34

98

Index

About the Author

Deborah DeEugenio holds a Doctor of Pharmacy degree from the University of the Sciences in Philadelphia, Philadelphia College of Pharmacy. She completed a post- doctoral residency in pharmacy practice at Thomas Jefferson University Hospital. Dr. DeEugenio is a Board Certified Pharmacotherapy Specialist and a Certified Anticoagulation Provider. Dr. DeEugenio is currently an Assistant Professor at Temple University School of Pharmacy in Philadelphia. She also works at Thomas Jefferson University Hospital as a clinical pharmacist for Jefferson Heart Institute and Jefferson Antithrombotics Therapy Service.

Debra Henn holds a Doctor of Pharmacy degree from the University of the Sciences in Philadelphia, Philadelphia College of Pharmacy. She completed a post-doctoral specialty residency in drug information at Thomas Jefferson University Hospital in Philadelphia and Bristol-Myers Squibb Company, Plainsboro New Jersey. Dr. Henn is currently employed as a Medical Information Manager at AstraZeneca Pharmaceuticals in Wilmington, Delaware.

About the Editor

David J. Triggle is a University Professor and a Distinguished Professor in the School of Pharmacy and Pharmaceutical Sciences at the State University of New York at Buffalo. He studied in the United Kingdom and earned his B.Sc. degree in Chemistry from the University of Southampton and a Ph.D. degree in Chemistry at the University of Hull. Following post-doctoral work at the University of Ottawa in Canada and the University of London in the United Kingdom, he assumed a position at the School of Pharmacy at Buffalo. He served as Chairman of the Department of Biochemical Pharmacology from 1971 to 1985 and as Dean of the School of Pharmacy from 1985 to 1995. From 1995 to 2001 he served as the Dean of the Graduate School, and as the University Provost from 2000 to 2001. He is the author of several books dealing with the chemical pharmacology of the autonomic nervous system and drug-receptor interactions, some 400 scientific publications, and has delivered more than 1,000 lectures worldwide on his research.